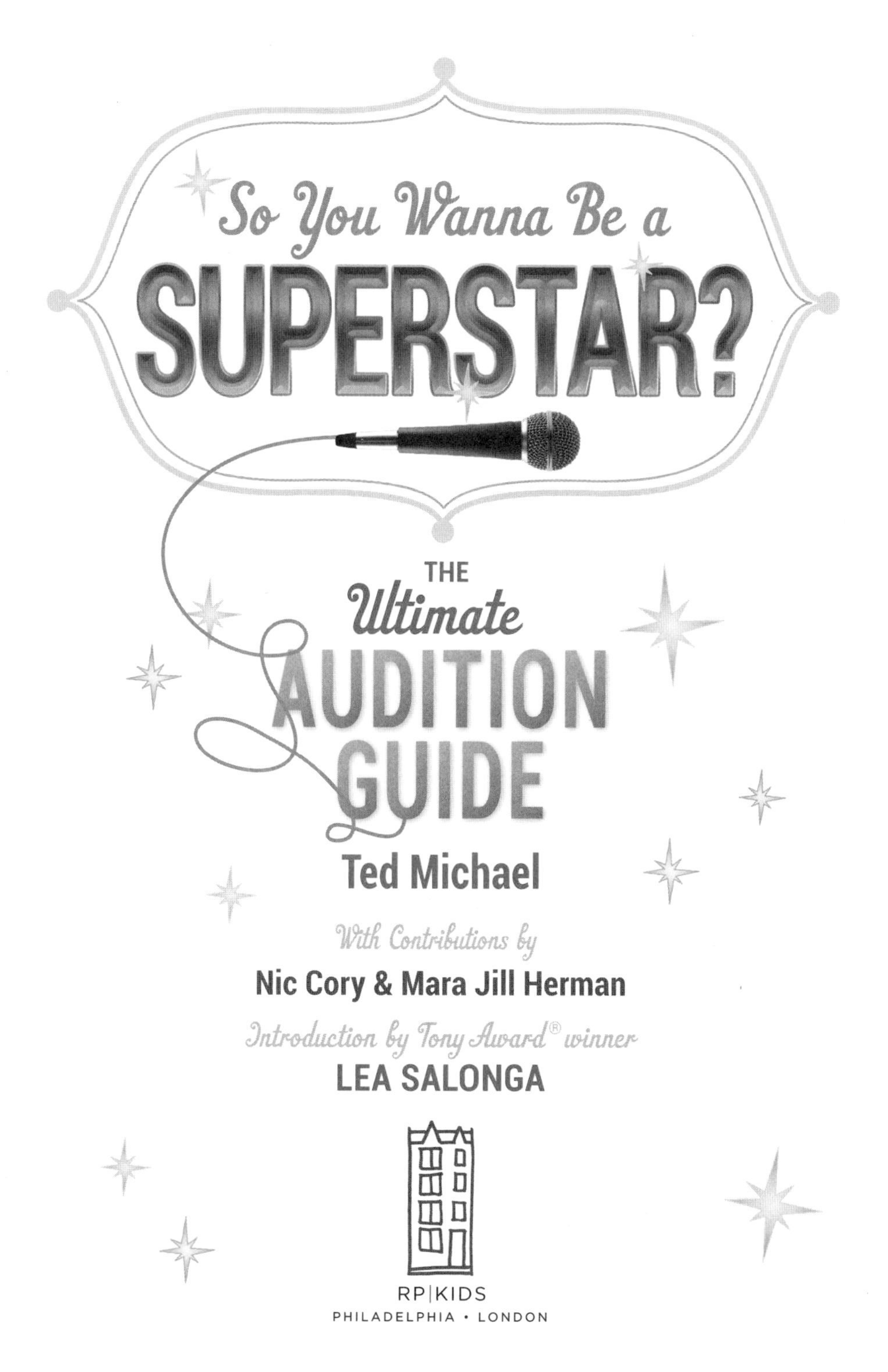
So You Wanna Be a
SUPERSTAR?
THE
Ultimate
AUDITION
GUIDE
Ted Michael
With Contributions by
Nic Cory & Mara Jill Herman
Introduction by Tony Award® winner
LEA SALONGA
RP|KIDS
PHILADELPHIA • LONDON

DEDICATION

To Nina Pfeffer, Louise Carmon, and Jeff Maynard, who helped us find our inner superstars.

—T. M., N. C., and M. J. H.

Printed in China

ISBN 978-0-7624-4610-0
Library of Congress Control Number: 2012932845
E-book ISBN 978-0-7624-4701-5

9 8 7 6 5 4 3 2 1
Digit on the right indicates the number of this printing

Designed by Frances J. Soo Ping Chow
Edited by Lisa Cheng
Typography: Archer, Budmo Jiggler, Dusseldorf, Gravitas One, HT Gelateria, Lobster Two, and Roboto

Published by Running Press Kids
An Imprint of Running Press Book Publishers
A Member of the Perseus Books Group
2300 Chestnut Street
Philadelphia, PA 19103–4371

Visit us on the web!
www.runningpress.com

Credits

Microphone: cover, p.8: iStock/Cole Vineyard
Stage light: p.14: iStock/Giedrius Dagys
Director's chair: p26: iStock/hero30
Disguise glasses: p.38: iStock/dtimiraos
Director's megaphone: p50: iStock/Rob Geddes
Ballet shoes: p.60: iStock/Soren Pilman
Mirror: p72: iStock/Rouzes
Slate and film reel: p94: iStock/kutay tanir
Theater masks: p106: iStock/Mehmet Salih Guler
Tickets: p128: iStock/ixer

CONTENTS

Overture . . . 4

CHAPTER ONE: Got Talent? . . . 8

CHAPTER TWO: Discovering Yourself . . . 14

CHAPTER THREE: Chatting About Craft . . . 26

CHAPTER FOUR: The Material Matters . . . 38

CHAPTER FIVE: Show Choirs and Glee Clubs . . . 50

CHAPTER SIX: The Dance Call . . . 60

CHAPTER SEVEN: I'm Ready for My Close-Up . . . 72

CHAPTER EIGHT: Warming Up . . . 84

CHAPTER NINE: How to Be Professional . . . 94

CHAPTER TEN: Dealing with Disappointment . . . 106

CHAPTER ELEVEN: Be Creative . . . 114

CHAPTER TWELVE: Backstage Pass . . . 128

Finale . . . 143

Encore . . . 144

Author's Note . . . 148

Acknowledgments . . . 150

About the Author and Contributors . . . 152

Overture

I can remember my first audition as if it happened just yesterday.

I was only six years old and was brought by my mother at the suggestion of her niece who was very active with a local repertory company. When it came my turn to get up and sing, I went up on the stage and sang "Do-Re-Mi" from *The Sound of Music*.

After I was done, the director (who was sitting right in front of the stage) asked me if I had a poem or a nursery rhyme that I could recite from memory. I said that I didn't know any poems, but that I did know my Girl Scout oath (my investiture happened a few weeks before, so I still had the oath memorized). She told me to go ahead. I then raised my hand in the Girl Scout salute, and proceeded to recite.

After that was done, I then shouted to my mother, "Mom, how did I do?"

The director then said, "You did fine. Now get off the stage."

I got hired.

Every performer knows that an audition is, by definition, a possibility. A chance.

Maybe you'll walk into a room, sing a song, and your life will change: You'll get cast in a show or land a coveted spot in a glee club or talent show. Your dream will come true.

Or maybe you'll walk into a room, sing a song, and then go back to your regular life, waiting for the next audition to come around.

Even for the most seasoned performers, lots of things are out of your control: What show or group are you auditioning for? Have you worked with anyone on the creative team before? Have any of the other parts been cast, and do you need to have chemistry with those performers?

So why not focus on what *is* in your control: Did you get a good night's sleep and eat a healthy breakfast? Did you memorize your lines for your monologue? Have you warmed up your voice so that you'll be ready to sing?

Everyone has to start somewhere—even superstars.

When I think back to my audition for *Miss Saigon*, I remember what a different experience that was from my first audition at six. . . . I was seventeen years old, a premed student in university, and completely terrified.

I had prepared "On My Own" from *Les Misérables* as my audition piece. When it came my turn to sing, I headed into the room where Cameron Mackintosh (Producer), Nicholas Hytner (Director), Alain Boublil (Lyricist), Claude-Michel Schönberg (Composer), Vinnie Liff (Casting Director), and James Thane (one of Cameron's associates from Australia) were waiting, seated behind a table.

I shook everyone's hand, and then stood on the X on the floor. The pianist began to play . . . but something was wrong. His tempo was too slow. So the entire song was sung way too slow. I tried very hard to hide the panic that was coursing through my veins, but beyond that, I tried to hide the worry that I would mess up this audition and lose my chance at getting cast. After I finished, Claude-Michel got up from his chair, played a few bars of "On My Own," and asked if I could sing the high part (I guess, just to check if I could). He then went back to his seat.

Nick then asked if I had prepared another song. I didn't, but knew of another song that I could do, a cappella if I needed to. I told them that I could sing "The Greatest Love of All" which was at this point in time extremely popular, thanks to Whitney Houston. I headed to the piano to ask the accompanist if he could play it for me.

I then spotted some sheet music sitting on top of the piano. My curiosity got the better of me, and lo and behold, it was sheet music for "The Greatest Love of All." So

I handed it to the piano man and said, "Here, play this."

Back to the X on the floor I went, praying all the while, hoping that the song would be in my key. Once the piano started to play, I knew that it was right. I then sang the song from start to finish.

I got hired.

Of course, these are only two examples out of many. No matter what happens on the day of an actual audition, you must prepare. Experience in musicals, show choirs, and talent shows at an early age will help you learn how to sing, how to be part of a musical "team," and what to expect when you're working on a show—either behind the scenes or right in the spotlight.

In this book you will find fun and valuable information about how to identify what your talents are, focus on your goals, and achieve success. Because being a superstar isn't just about being a good performer—it's about doing your research, practicing your craft, and, above all, believing in yourself and knowing that your dreams can come true.

Lea Salonga

CHAPTER ONE
Got Talent?

o you wanna be a superstar? Work hard and never give up. You'll probably hear "no"more than you will "yes," but that will make the yes's that much more exciting. Perform as much as you can, because experience will make you a better actor, singer, and dancer. Take voice lessons and dance classes. Go to the theater, volunteer at one if you can. Seriously consider higher education and spending four years focusing on becoming better at your craft. Make the investment now so it can pay off big-time in the future.

—JOSH PULTZ, SENIOR TALENT AGENT, DGRW TALENT INC.

Welcome!

Chances are, if you're reading this book then you're interested in auditioning for your school musical, talent show, or glee club.

Now, you may think that all auditions come down to one thing—talent. And in a way, that's true. *Talent* is defined as:

the potential for success; ability

Notice that the definition isn't that you must have "a really freaking awesome voice." Talent isn't that specific. The words to focus on are potential and ability—the willingness to learn about your craft, studying and practicing, and (most of all) understanding that everyone's talent is *different*. If you compare yourself to others, you'll only get frustrated. Instead, focus on you and what *you* do best.

This isn't easy, of course.

Especially in school, being different can be a casualty—a reason to get made fun of or be excluded.

On stage, however, being different is an asset. As a performer, your quirky habits, individual skills, and even how you look make you special and help you stand out.

Take singing, for example. If you watch *American Idol*, not everyone is classically trained and wants to be an opera singer. There are pop singers who have never taken a singing lesson but have extraordinary "raw" talent.

There are country singers who play the guitar.

R&B singers who show off their vocal pyrotechnics—switching quickly from note to note in incredibly impressive ways.

Rock singers who may not sound "pretty" but wow audiences with how powerful their voices are, and the intensity of their performances.

There are belters.

There are sopranos.

There are boys who can sing in falsetto.

All of this and more—and if some of these words or concepts are unfamiliar to you now, don't worry. They'll be explained in future chapters. The important thing to remember is that no one kind of performer is "better" than another. At the end of the day, superstardom all comes down to dedication and practice.

The Superstar Checklist

Did you read any of the above descriptions and think, "Hey, this sounds a lot like me!"

Whatever your background is, that's okay. Here's a checklist to figure out what your talent is and how to start making the most of it.

Name: ______________________________

Age: ______________________________

Favorite Activity: ______________________________

Instruments I Can Play: ______________________________

I would rather (mark one):

○ Act ○ Sing ○ Dance ○ Play an Instrument

Favorite Singer(s): ______________________________

____

Favorite Actor(s): ______________________________

____

Favorite Band(s): ______________________________

____

Have you ever written a song?	Yes	No
If not, would you like to?	Yes	No
Have you ever taken a dance lesson?	Yes	No
If not, would you like to?	Yes	No
Have you ever taken a voice lesson?	Yes	No
If not, would you like to?	Yes	No
Have you ever taken an instrument lesson?	Yes	No
If not, would you like to?	Yes	No
Have you ever performed in front of an audience?	Yes	No

If so, how many people?________________________________

Do you ever get nervous before you perform?	Yes	No

What is your performing "dream"?____________________________

____

____

____

Now it's time to look over your answers. Hopefully, they'll help you start to discover what kind of superstar you'd like to be.

Oftentimes, we admire people who we'd like to emulate. For example, whomever you listed as your favorite singers might tell us what kind of singer you'd like to be.

Did you write down Pink or Kelly Clarkson? Maybe you'd like to be a pop star and perform some of your favorite songs in your school's show choir.

Did you write Brian Stokes Mitchell or Jonathan Groff? You might want to be a leading man on Broadway.

Then it's time to mix and match.

Is your favorite performing artist Taylor Swift? Do you know how to play the guitar—or if you don't, would you like to learn how? Perhaps becoming a singer/songwriter is in your future.

Do you like Coldplay or the Beatles? And do you play an instrument like the drums or the piano? Why not get together with some of your friends and start a band?

Love to dance? You can be a dancer in a musical, or even a music video on MTV. Or maybe you don't want to be on stage yourself. You could become a choreographer, and create routines for your friends to perform in the school talent show, or record and put up on YouTube. They could even get on *So You Think You Can Dance?* or *America's Got Talent*.

The point? Dream big, because you never know what can happen.

But first you have to have a goal. Once you figure out *what* you're passionate about, you'll be able to take the first step to becoming the superstar you were born to be.

So take a good look at the answers you just wrote down, because within these pages you will learn how to prepare for an audition and be the very best that you can be. You'll learn the smartest (and easiest) ways to research the upcoming school or community show, how to choose audition material for your school's talent show that will showcase your strengths instead of your weaknesses, insider tips and tricks on how to impress the director while keeping your nerves in check, and what to do once the dreaded audition is over and all that's left to do is *wait*.

Whether you're a total newbie, a seasoned vet, or somewhere in between, everything you need to know about auditioning is right here. For your eyes only.

So sit back, relax, and enjoy the ~~show~~ book!

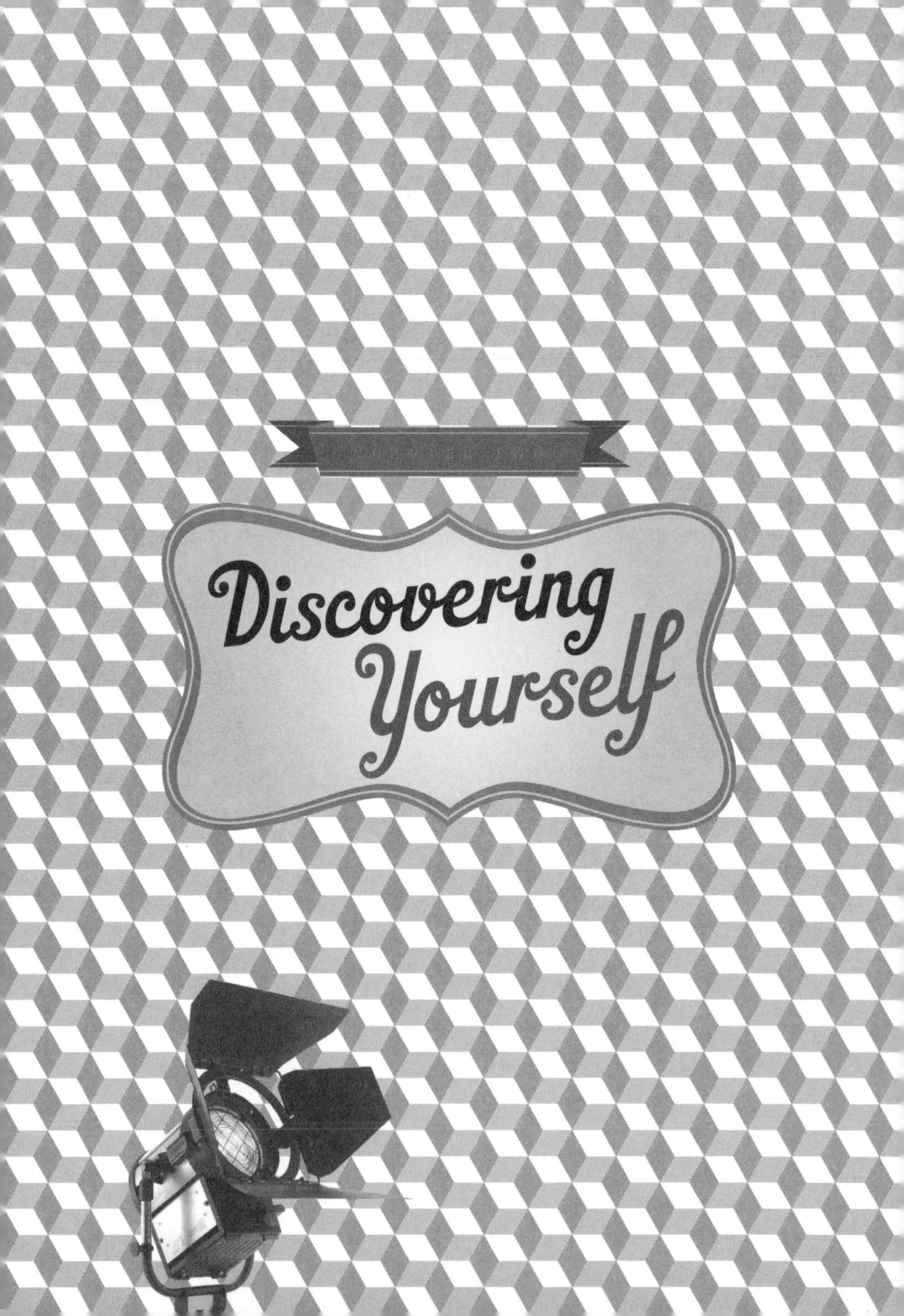

Discovering Yourself

For me, the idea of being a superstar is about remembering that there are many definitions of the word. Of course there's someone who gets to be in a Broadway show and gets to be a part of all that glitter and excitement (and that's cool, don't get me wrong). But there's also understanding that not everyone will get to do that and realizing that they're not going to die if they don't. There are so many ways to take the gift that you have and share it with the world. . . . There's regional theater, local choir, community theater, church, and Teaching (which gets a capital T), to name a few. Broadway's in one location, but living a life in NYC is not for everyone, and you can take your gift anywhere and use it for good in so many ways and you just might discover that being a superstar to a neighbor or a kid is just as fulfilling as what you dream of at night.

—JULIA MURNEY, ACCLAIMED AWARD WINNER
FOR ELPHABA IN *WICKED* (NATIONAL TOUR/BROADWAY) AND
DRAMA DESK NOMINEE FOR QUEENIE IN *THE WILD PARTY*

iguring out who you are can be a difficult task, but the easiest way to start is with a mirror.

Are you tall? Short? Fair? Dark? Lean? Shapely? Make a list of all of your physical characteristics, and don't judge what you see. Keep it nice and simple. Here's an example:

I have brown eyes.

I have short black hair.

I have long legs.

I have tiny arms.

Treat this exercise as if you've just made a new friend and you want to learn everything about him or her. What's the first thing you notice? Write it down. What stands out? Write it down.

My Physical Traits

____________________ ____________________

____________________ ____________________

____________________ ____________________

____________________ ____________________

____________________ ____________________

____________________ ____________________

Hello, you, I'd like to introduce you to YOU!

Your physical characteristics will help determine the types of roles you're going to play. You are fabulous and unique and there is only one of you—so, don't fight what you're working with. Embrace it!

I Am What I Am

(*La Cage aux Folles*, 1983)

While physical traits are important, your personality is your calling card: Are you naturally funny? Serious? Loud or quiet? Do you follow the rules—or do you like to break them?

Write down the character traits you know to be true about yourself. Again, be as honest as possible.

My Personality Traits

____________________	____________________
____________________	____________________
____________________	____________________
____________________	____________________
____________________	____________________
____________________	____________________

If you're having a hard time with this exercise, try asking a friend or family member whose opinion you trust.

Remember, the goal is to figure out what types of characters you could play most naturally. It doesn't mean that you won't play a serious character if you're the class clown. You'll probably get all types of roles over the course of your career.

The Music of My Soul

(*Memphis*, 2009)

Time to get a little more technical. Let's start by figuring out your voice type.

Voice types are usually divided into five categories. From lowest to highest, they are: bass, baritone, tenor, mezzo-soprano (sometimes referred to as "alto"), and soprano. Funny names, right? They're Italian. If you're a boy, you're probably a bass, baritone, or tenor. Girls typically fall into mezzo-soprano or soprano.

Most voices don't reach full maturity until a singer is in his/her late twenties. But this should give you an idea of what you'll be working with soon enough.

Listed after each voice part are examples of famous singers from the musical theater and pop worlds who would be classified as such.

BASS: The lowest of all the voice types. Basses are usually the oldest and most robust male roles in a musical.

Pop: Alex Band (The Calling), Johnny Cash, Barry White

Musical Theater: Chuck Cooper, Michael Cerveris, Paul Robeson

BARITONE: The most common male voice. Roles can include everything from the comedic sidekick to the romantic lead to the evil villain.

Pop: Adam Levine (Maroon 5), Elvis, Frank Sinatra, Jim Morrison (The Doors)

Musical Theater: John Gallagher Jr., Norbert Leo Butz, Brian Stokes Mitchell

TENOR: The highest male voice. Most tenor roles are the romantic leads in a musical.

Pop: Justin Bieber, Bruno Mars, Adam Lambert, Cee Lo Green, Elton John

Musical Theater: Jonathan Groff, Matthew Morrison, Gavin Creel, Aaron Tveit

MEZZO-SOPRANO: Most "belting," a style of singing that mixes the head and chest voices, is done in the mezzo range. Mezzos, like baritones, are a pretty versatile category of singers. They can play anything from the funny best friend to the quirky leading lady to the meanest girl on stage.

Pop: Selena Gomez, Adele, Pink, Katy Perry, Lady Gaga

Musical Theater: Sutton Foster, Idina Menzel, Patti LuPone, Lea Michele

SOPRANO: The highest of the vocal ranges. These ladies are usually the romantic leads. However, sometimes composers allow them to show their darker side by making them the high-pitched villains in a musical show.

Pop: Mariah Carey, Whitney Houston, Christina Aguilera, Beyoncé

Musical Theater: Kristin Chenoweth, Kelli O'Hara, Audra McDonald

NOTE: Lots of famous singers have remarkably wide ranges. Individual voices often don't fit neatly into one vocal classification. The examples given are indications of the music—and corresponding vocal range—for which the singers are best known.

Need more help to determine your voice part?

Go to your local library and take out a few cast recordings. Then sing along—there will be some characters whom you can hit the same notes as. That means you're probably the same voice part.

Search online or ask a friend what "voice types" the singers who play these parts are, and voilà!

TIP: You're better off listening to a more "classic" Broadway show like *Oklahoma!* or *Camelot* because the voice parts are easier to distinguish. In shows like

Spring Awakening or *Legally Blonde*, it's harder to tell.

You can also figure your voice part out from listening to contemporary artists on the radio. Justin Timberlake, for example, is *definitely* a tenor, while Sarah McLachlan is a soprano for sure.

iTunes

Unless you're living under a rock, you probably know most of the songs on the *Billboard* Hot 100—they're featured in the hottest movies, and your best friends play them on their iPods during lunch. However, one great way to find more obscure material and unknown artists is to go to a little place called iTunes.

Don't just buy all the #1 singles. Buy your favorite artist's *complete* album in order to mine new material that nobody else will even think of singing.

Use the "Genius" feature on iTunes to get suggestions of other artists and songs you might like. The more research you do, the better shot you have at finding that perfect song and nailing your big audition!

The Diva's Lament

(*Monty Python's Spamalot*, 2005)

Types are more than just how high (or low) you can sing, though.

Types are about *attitude*, and everyone knows who has the most attitude in musical theater: a diva.

A diva is typically defined as such:

a very successful singer

But being a diva is much more than that—it's a way of life. A diva can be male or female, short or tall, rotund or compact.

In our society, a diva can sometimes have a negative connotation: drama queen. And while most performers can be a little, well, *dramatic*, that's a very small part of being a true diva. A little sass is okay as long as you're not being rude.

But really, the most important—and defining—feature of a diva isn't talent or skill or having a personal assistant. It's self-confidence.

WARNING: Being confident doesn't mean being rude.

A true diva treats others how he or she wants to be treated; when it comes to performing, what goes around comes around. There's never a place for name-calling or cruelty in the arts, and it's important not to be selfish. You want your moment in the spotlight, but so does everyone else—and more than just one person deserves a chance to shine. A diva knows when to speak up and share an idea or suggestion, but also when to respect the artistic vision of others.

Lastly, a true diva puts the good of the show before him- or herself. Sometimes this isn't the easiest thing to do, but it's what will create the best piece of art—and at the end of the day, *that* is what matters most.

POP QUIZ:

How Diva Are You?

Below is a simple quiz to determine your level of diva-rocity. Answer each question completely honestly. If you don't, the only person you're fooling is yourself.

1. It's the first day of auditions for your school musical, and you realize someone else is wearing the exact same outfit. The first thing you do is:

A) Grab spare clothes from your locker (you always keep a backup outfit ready just in case) and run into the bathroom to change. You wouldn't be caught dead wearing identical duds as someone else.

B) Approach that person and demand he/she be the one to change—not you.

C) Spill your drink all over him or her. This way, the person will have no other choice but to change. Mission accomplished.

D) Do nothing. Who cares if someone is wearing the same clothes? It's talent that counts, and you've got it in abundance.

2. Your arch nemesis overhears you telling your friend what monologue you're performing for your audition. You:

A) Worry that your nemesis will be performing the same monologue, but it's too late to learn anything new. Hopefully you'll score the part regardless.

B) Immediately learn another monologue. You can't even risk the chance that your nemesis will try and outdo you.

C) Have your friend snoop around and find out what monologue your nemesis is doing. You're too busy preparing to do the snooping yourself.

D) Who cares? You purposely lied to your friend about what monologue you're performing in the first place to throw your nemesis off track.

3. The director announces this year's musical, and you're totally peeved because you're not right for any of the parts. You:

A) Don't audition. The only part worth playing is a lead, and since you won't get one, you'd rather spend your time doing something else completely.

B) March into your director's office and complain. You're the best one in school—he better pick a new show or else.

C) Cry and ask your mom to call the principal. Surely the director is out to get you, and if anyone can solve this problem, it's your mother.

D) Audition anyway. It's not the size of the part that matters, its being involved in a show and spending time with your fellow thespians.

4. The high note in your solo is way too high, and you crack every time you rehearse. You:

A) Keep on trying. Surely with enough practice you'll get it eventually.

B) Ask one of the girls in the ensemble who can hit the note to sing it from backstage. This way you'll stay true to the composer's vision, which is more important than your ego.

C) Decide to sing a lower note. It won't be as fierce, but it's better than embarrassing yourself in front of the entire school.

D) Request that the music director transpose the music down half a step so you can hit the note, even though this means he will have to reorchestrate the entire number by hand, which could take days.

5. You have your first costume fitting, and it's way too tight. You:

A) Immediately go on a diet—you've gotta lose five pounds by opening night!

B) Throw a fit and run out the door screaming. The costume designer is obviously out to get you.

C) Ask the costume designer to let the seams out. It would be nice to lose some weight, but you don't believe in starving yourself.

D) Sneak into school after rehearsal and rip up the costume. Who cares if it took hours and hours to sew? Now the designer will have to make a new one, and this time you better believe it will fit.

6. There's simply no spark between you and your love interest in the show. You decide to:

A) Get a haircut and make sure you look your best for the next rehearsal—maybe there's something wrong with you!

B) Spend more time with him or her. If you get to know each other outside of rehearsal, maybe that will help create some chemistry.

C) Do nothing. It's all about you, right? So what if there's no chemistry as long as *you* give the performance of a lifetime.

D) Complain to the director—obviously this other kid has to go.

7. It's one week before the show opens, and you still don't have all your lines memorized. You:

A) Aren't worried. You're a good performer. You'll know your lines by opening night.

B) Stay home Friday night instead of hanging out with your friends. Learning your lines is more important right now than having fun.

C) Laugh when the director yells at you. If you don't know your lines, you'll just make them up.

D) Take your costume home with you and sew rhinestones all over it. That way, people will be so blinded by your costume they won't notice if you flub a line or not.

8. You find out someone in the cast is talking trash about you. Your immediate reaction is:

A) What? Why? Did I do something wrong?

B) Somebody is obviously jealous of me. How cute.

C) Who? Who would dare say anything rude about me?

D) Interesting. Good thing it's not true.

9. The show is running way too long, and the director decides to cut your favorite scene. You:

A) Breathe a sigh of relief. Now you can finally have a few minutes offstage to gather your thoughts before the finale.

B) Threaten to quit. This is ridiculous—you're the star of the show!

C) Speak your lines really fast. If the show is shorter, surely the director will put your scene back in.

D) Are in complete shock. Your scene is the best one in the show. You ask the director to reconsider.

10. It's opening night and you're sick. You:

A) Ask the director to make an announcement beforehand letting the audience know you're sick. This way, if you mess up, they'll (hopefully) understand.

B) Don't show up. Without you, they'll have to cancel the show. Yeah, it will piss people off, but what's more important: having friends or having people think you're untalented?

C) Suck it up and deal. You don't have an understudy, and—as they say—the show must go on.

D) Pay someone in the ensemble to go on in your place.

SCORE

Now that you've answered the questions to the best of your ability, go back and add up how many points you have using the key below.

1.
A) 4
B) 2
C) 3
D) 1
Points: ____

2.
A) 1
B) 2
C) 3
D) 4
Points: ____

3.
A) 3
B) 4
C) 2
D) 1
Points: ____

4.
A) 1
B) 3
C) 2
D) 4
Points: ____

5.
A) 1
B) 3
C) 2
D) 4
Points: ____

6.
A) 1
B) 2
C) 4
D) 3
Points: ____

7.
A) 2
B) 1
C) 4
D) 3
Points: ____

8.
A) 1
B) 4
C) 3
D) 2
Points: ____

9.
A) 1
B) 4
C) 3
D) 2
Points: ____

10.
A) 3
B) 4
C) 1
D) 2
Points: ____

Total Points: ____

KEY

NOT A DIVA (10–15 points): You care about theater, but you also care about doing the right thing. You are a "nice" person, but nobody ever said divas were nice, did they? Focus on stepping up and sharing your ideas—you have a lot of important things to say!

DIVA-ISH (16–24 points): You still care about what others think of you and your moment in the spotlight, but you're starting to realize you may have to share that spotlight—and that's okay.

DIVA-IN-TRAINING (25–34 points): You *want* to be a diva, but you're not there just yet. You tend to throw tantrums instead of acting fairly and understanding that you can't always get your way. Practice makes perfect, but beware—you want to be a diva, not just *mean*.

DIVA SUPREME (35–40 points): Congratulations! You, my friend, are a diva. The perfect mix of sassitude (sass + attitude), talent, and self-confidence.

CHAPTER THREE
Chatting About Craft

Me, I've always followed the Renaissance poet, Sir Philip Sidney's advice: "'Fool,' said my Muse to me, 'Look in thy heart and write.'" It was only through listening to my own heart, trusting my instinct, that I conceived such a harebrained scheme as turning a nineteenth-century German Expressionist play into the rock musical *Spring Awakening*. The conception of that show was also informed by my love and knowledge of both Greek tragedy and twentieth-century Modernist fiction. And this reflection leads to the second part of my advice, which is to immerse yourself in great authors, to make them your mentors in your craft. As for me, I never took a writing course. Rather, I turned to Shakespeare, Chaucer, Miton, Aeschylus, Chekhov, Beckett, Spenser. . . . These writers have had such a profound influence on me, that when I look to my heart, I find them there.

—STEVEN SATER, TONY AWARD WINNER
FOR BEST BOOK AND SCORE OF *SPRING AWAKENING*

It's time to meet the people behind the magic.

Let's start by defining the various types of theatrical writers. Musical writers can be divided into three categories: composers, lyricists, and librettists. Some writers focus on one area and allow collaborators to handle the other two, while others do everything themselves. Here's what each writer does:

The *composer* writes all of the music.

A *lyricist* writes all of the words in the songs.

The librettist writes the book of a musical, which comprises all of the scenes between the songs.

Pretty simple, right?

Musical theater writers have voices that are as unique as the actors who sing their work. As a performer, you should be able to know the difference between Stephen Sondheim and Stephen Schwartz, or Lynn Ahrens and Lin-Manuel Miranda.

The following list of musical writers is by no means comprehensive, but will help you get your feet wet.

GILBERT AND SULLIVAN:

What Ought We to Do?

(*The Pirates of Penzance*, 1879)

Although most contemporary musicals don't sound anything like the high-pitched wailing you'd hear in an opera house, their roots can be traced back to these two English blokes and their operettas. W. S. Gilbert wrote the words, and Arthur Sullivan wrote the music.

Operetta, by the way, can be translated to mean "little opera," but let's just call it

"Diet Opera." In other words, the stories are as fun and fluffy as those you might find in any light opera but without all of the drama. Their most popular musical stories include *H.M.S. Pinafore*, *The Gondoliers*, and *The Pirates of Penzance*. One of their operettas, *The Mikado*, even got a face-lift: *The Hot Mikado*, a jazz reinterpretation of the musical with orchestrations by Charles L. Cooke, played Broadway in 1939.

Random Trivia: Gilbert and Sullivan were known to argue. A lot. They even fought over carpet that was installed at the Savoy Theatre, where all of their works premiered. There were lawsuits, and it almost ended their partnership.

GEORGE AND IRA GERSHWIN:

Fascinating Rhythm

(Lady Be Good, 1924)

George Gershwin wrote the music, and Ira, his older brother, wrote the lyrics. The family duo penned over a dozen Broadway shows, everything from the first musical comedy to win the coveted Pulitzer Prize (*Of Thee I Sing*, 1931) to an operatic interpretation of African American life in South Carolina in the 1920s, *Porgy and Bess* (1935).

In their musical comedies, Ira's witty lyrics are set to George's musical combination of American jazz and ragtime. George was also an accomplished film and orchestral composer: his most famous work is probably *Rhapsody in Blue*, which he wrote for orchestra and piano.

Random Trivia: One of the musicals the Gershwin brothers wrote together, *Oh, Kay!*, was named after a lady friend of George's: the musician Kay Swift.

RODGERS & HART:

Bewitched, Bothered and Bewildered

(*Pal Joey*, 1940)

Richard Rodgers composed the memorable music that accompanied Lorenz Hart's famously clever and sophisticated lyrics. They met as students at Columbia University in New York City and collaborated on twenty-eight musicals and over five hundred songs. Some of their most famous collaborations are shows that feature lots of big dance numbers such as *On Your Toes* (1936), *Babes in Arms* (1937), and *Pal Joey* (1940).

Random Trivia: *Pal Joey* was dramatically too dark for Broadway when it premiered in 1940, because it centers on a protagonist who is not very likable. It wasn't until the musical was revived in the fifties—after Hart had died and Rodgers had moved on to work with his most successful partner, Oscar Hammerstein II—that the general public embraced the work as a classic.

RODGERS & HAMMERSTEIN:

I Whistle a Happy Tune

(*The King and I*, 1951)

You may be wondering: whatever happened to Rodgers and Hart?

Well, at one point Rodgers asked Oscar Hammerstein II to be his new lyrics-writing buddy for a project that would eventually become *Oklahoma!*, which Hart wasn't interested in working on. And it's a good thing he did, too, because they ushered in the Golden Age of Broadway with classic American musicals like *Carousel*

(1945), *South Pacific* (1949), *The King and I* (1951), and *The Sound of Music* (1959).

They revolutionized the art form by seamlessly integrating the acting, song, and dance in order to tell stories that were character-driven, dramatic, and socially relevant. Their song catalog has been endlessly interpreted by musical theater performers and also reimagined by jazz and pop singers—a testament to their enduring legacy as songwriters.

Chances are *you'll* do an R&H show. They're so darn memorable—who *didn't* learn to sing along with the von Trapp children while belting out "Do-Re-Mi"?

Random Trivia: In 2009, *Forbes* named Rodgers and Hammerstein the second "Top-Earning Deceased Celebrity" at $235 million. Who says there's no money to be made in theater?

LEONARD BERNSTEIN:

Conquering New York

(*Wonderful Town*, 1953)

Leonard Bernstein was an American composer known for his musicals and his orchestral music and conducting.

His collaborations with the lyric-writing duo of Betty Comden and Adolph Green yielded great successes in *On the Town* (1944) and *Wonderful Town* (1953). Arguably his greatest musical achievement was *West Side Story* (1957), which he wrote with a then-unknown lyricist named Stephen Sondheim. His music is rhythmically complex and dramatically charged; the listener never knows what will be coming next.

Random Trivia: Bernstein won sixteen Grammy Awards.

STEPHEN SONDHEIM:

God, That's Good!

(*Sweeney Todd*, 1979)

Few musical writers are as revered as Stephen Sondheim.

While his lyrics for *Gypsy* (1959) and *West Side Story* (1957) gained him notoriety as an unparalleled wordsmith, Sondheim eventually decided to pursue his passion for writing lyrics *and* music. His penchant for unexpected subject matter, dark humor, and haunting melodies, and a handful of songs that have been chart-toppers in the popular music world have secured his spot as one of the most influential musical writers of all time.

Major works include *A Funny Thing Happened on the Way to the Forum* (1962), *Company* (1970), *A Little Night Music* (1973), *Sunday in the Park with George* (1984), and *Into the Woods* (1987).

Random Trivia: Sondheim wrote the music and lyrics for Warren Beatty's movie *Dick Tracy* (1990). One of the songs, "Sooner or Later (I Always Get My Man)," was performed by Madonna and won Sondheim an Academy Award.

KANDER & EBB:

A Tough Act to Follow

(*Curtains*, 2006)

Fred Ebb wrote lyrics—up until his death in 2004—to John Kander's music. Their songs are remarkably memorable, and their musical subject matter includes everything from a naughty watering hole in Nazi Germany (*Cabaret*, 1966) to a group of wrongly convicted African American males in the American South (*The Scottsboro Boys*, 2010).

A couple of their musicals have been successfully adapted into award-winning films, including *Cabaret* (1972), which starred Liza Minnelli, and *Chicago* (2002).

Random Trivia: Kander and Ebb wrote one of the most famous musical-turned-popular songs ever written, "New York, New York," for Martin Scorsese's movie of the same name. It has since been recorded by many musical icons, including Sammy Davis Jr., Queen, Reel Big Fish, Michael Bublé, and even Beyoncé.

ANDREW LLOYD WEBBER:

And the Money Kept Rolling In (and Out)

(*Evita*, 1976)

There is no musical theater composer living today who is as famous—or wealthy—as Sir Andrew Lloyd Webber.

His success started with the lyricist Tim Rice and their collaborations on *Joseph and the Amazing Technicolor Dreamcoat* (1968) and *Jesus Christ Superstar* (1970). Next came *Evita*, which tells the story of Argentinean dictator Eva Perón; *Cats* about, well, cats in 1981; and *Starlight Express* in 1984, which requires actors to wear roller skates. But his most popular musical by far is *The Phantom of the Opera* (1986), which has been seen by over 100 million people.

Random Trivia: Webber's second marriage was to singer and actress Sarah Brightman, whom he cast as the first Christine Daaé, the fragile soprano leading lady in *The Phantom of the Opera*. Even after giving her a "big break," they divorced in 1990.

STEPHEN SCHWARTZ:

It's an Art

(*Working*, 1978)

A composer and lyricist of many memorable musicals—and even an opera—Stephen Schwartz has worked not only on stage productions but also several films, including writing lyrics for the Disney classics *Pocahontas* (1995), *The Hunchback of Notre Dame* (1996), and *Enchanted* (2007).

His songs bridge the gap between musical theater and the pop/rock world with high-stakes drama and driving music that showcase all of the "money notes" performers love to show off in auditions. Some of his most famous works include *Godspell* (1971), *Pippin* (1972), *Children of Eden* (1991), and the one about witches that you can probably recite by heart, *Wicked* (2003).

Random Trivia: Stephen Schwartz has even written rock music. The composer collaborated with the rock singer-songwriter John Ondrasik of Five for Fighting on *Slice*, the band's fifth studio album. Ondrasik approached Schwartz after his daughter became an avid fan of *Wicked*.

AHRENS & FLAHERTY:

New Music

(*Ragtime*, 1996)

Lynn Ahrens and Stephen Flaherty met at the BMI Lehman Engel Musical Theatre Writing Workshop—a breeding ground for successful collaborations—in 1982 and still write together today.

Their musicals and songs are ethnically diverse: They've written about everything from a native girl turning into a tree (*Once on This Island*, 1990) to an Irish theater group determined to stage a production of Oscar Wilde's *Salome* in *A Man of No Importance* (2002), and created a musical collection of beloved Dr. Seuss stories (*Seussical*, 2000) as well as a Russian-influenced animated film score about a young girl who turns out to be a princess (*Anastasia*, 1997).

Random Trivia: Lynn Ahrens wrote and sang several original product jingles, including: "What Would You Do for a Klondike Bar?" and "Bounty: The Quilted, Quicker Picker-Upper."

JONATHAN LARSON:
Louder Than Words

(*tick, tick ... BOOM!*, 2001)

For those of us who can't recite *Rent* (1996) by heart, here's some information on this composer/lyricist who died way too young: Jonathan Larson's music is influenced by the rock and grunge styles that were popular when he was writing during the late eighties and early-to-mid-nineties. The line between pop music and musical theater is totally blurred in Larson's music, which he performed with a rock band as his backup. *Rent* is an adaptation of Puccini's opera *La Bohème*, and tells the tragic story of two ill-fated lovers.

Random Trivia: Stephen Sondheim was a mentor to Jonathan Larson and a huge fan of his work. He even wrote several letters of recommendation for Larson, who ended up winning the Stephen Sondheim Award.

JASON ROBERT BROWN:

You Don't Know This Man

(*Parade*, 1998)

Jason Robert Brown established himself as a composer to watch in 1995 with the pop-influenced sounds of his *Songs for a New World*. His signature style is especially *patter-y*, meaning that the singing sounds almost like talking in the narrow range of notes used in the verses and the clipped pace at which the characters "sing." But don't let this fool you; the songs often grow into ministories that feature lots of pop belting and *melisma*—the technical term for riffing.

Some of his most famous works include *Parade* (1998), about the wrongful execution of a Jewish man in the deep South; *The Last Five Years* (2001), which tells the story of a romantic relationship both from beginning-to-end and from end-to-beginning; and *13* (2007), about a boy who moves from New York to Indiana as he is about to celebrate his Bar Mitzvah.

Random Trivia: Brown was a camper at French Woods Festival, a performing arts summer camp that boasts some pretty remarkable alumni like actresses Zooey Deschanel and Melissa Errico, fashion designer Zac Posen, and Maroon 5's Adam Levine.

For additional information about the composers and lyricists listed above, as well as many other musical makers, watch the PBS documentary *Broadway: The American Musical*. It covers the evolution of the Broadway musical from 1893 to 2004. The companion book by Michael Kantor and Laurence Maslon is also a great read for those interested in musical theater history.

Express Yourself

(Madonna, 1989)

Let's not forget about pop music.

If you're auditioning for your school's glee club, you'll probably be required to know a little something about the singer-songwriters who rule the airwaves. While some artists may be great performers, they don't necessarily write all their own music. Instead, they often have big teams of music executives who plot their songs, draft their albums, and Auto-Tune their voices.

However, there are a handful of current composer-lyricists who write at least some of the music they perform. These artists include Lady Gaga, Ke$ha, Adele, Bruno Mars, and Cee Lo Green. They remind us of the good old days when it was generally expected that singers could and would write most of their own songs. Legends such as James Taylor, Joni Mitchell, and the Beatles wrote the majority of the music they recorded and performed.

There is a very fine line between good performers and great artists. Try to find singers whose music you like to perform and who actually write their own music. It may take a while, but you'll be surprised with the options you find. Because while there's nothing wrong with having someone else write your material, there *is* something extra special about choosing material that comes from the pen of an artist you respect and admire.

The Material Matters

Go to the theater, study, and stay connected to your friends and family (as they will be your grounding constant). Fake it till ya make it! No one is utterly confident—those who succeed and work consistently are those who have learned how to convincingly "act" confident. Seriously! Be yourself, not who you think "they" want you to be—because ultimately, neither you nor they know what they want until they see it in someone authentically. Don't beat yourself up. It's a numbers game. Realize that if you stick it out, you will eventually work. And that if you don't book the job, it's not personal, has nothing actually to do with you, who you are as a quality human being. Know that the material you choose to present yourself with in an audition tells people who you are, so look for things that are not overdone, make you feel excited about performing, and truly speak to your core. And last but not least, always perform for *yourself* (not the people behind the audition table, the audience, whomever)! When you are really "inside" a scene or song and transported by your own joy at performing it, those watching you will be as well.

—EMILY SKINNER, TONY NOMINEE AND
DRAMA LEAGUE AWARD RECIPIENT FOR *SIDE SHOW*

Choosing the right material for your audition is an integral part of your success. In fact, the material you choose can either make or break your audition.

So, how do you do it? Let's start at the very beginning—a very good place to start. Hey, if it's good enough for the von Trapp children, it's good enough for you.

A Trip to the Library

(*She Loves Me*, 1963)

Do your research!

If there is a script or libretto floating around your local or school library, check it out! If there's a movie version of the show, grab a bag of popcorn and watch it!

FACT: Familiarizing yourself with the show you'll be auditioning for will help inform what audition material you will need to prepare.

Once you do this, start talking to yourself. Find out just how well you understand the story by asking yourself basic plot-related questions, such as: Who is in love with whom? When did they fall for each other? What does the villain want from the protagonist? Who gets to belt the highest note?

Okay, that last question was a joke. But the other ones are serious, quiz-worthy questions! As someone who is about to be in a musical, you need to be able to answer any query about the make-believe world you're about to call home.

Putting It Together

(*Sunday in the Park with George*, 1984)

Now that you understand the world of the musical, it's time to figure out how you fit into it. What role do you want and just how are you going to get it?

GENDER BENDER

There are lots of productions out there that reinvent the way musical theater is performed. Many of these include nontraditional, gender-defying casting. In other words, sometimes boys play girls on Broadway. And vice versa.

However, unless you're auditioning at a very progressive high school or an extremely edgy community theater, the boy actors will probably play men and the girls will be women. Taking that into account, choose an audition piece that was written for someone of your gender. That way, you're giving yourself the best shot at landing one of the roles the director is realistically considering you for.

Of course, there are always exceptions to the rule. For example, look at the song "The Man That Got Away," sung by the incomparable Judy Garland in *A Star Is Born*. Lots of men, including Bobby Darin, Jeff Buckley, and even Frank Sinatra have covered that song since Judy sang it on the big screen. A slight alteration of the lyrics to make it more gender appropriate is totally okay—just as long as you're maintaining its emotional integrity.

Promptly familiarize yourself with the songs that each character sings so that you can match your vocal range with the appropriate *track*—another term for role or a set of multiple roles—in the show.

Which role in this particular musical is best for you? Are you the ingénue? What about the comic sidekick? A sultry lover, perhaps?

Of course, we'd all like to be the lead—and at some point in your career, you probably will be. But you should always be honest with yourself about the roles you are *right* for in this particular production. By setting your sights on a specific role, you will better be able to choose appropriate material that will help you ace your audition!

Sing!

(*A Chorus Line*, 1975)

One of the most important ways to tell if you're right for a particular role is whether or not you can sing it.

Not some of it, but all of it. And live to tell the tale.

Singing a role does not mean praying with all your heart that you will maybe, almost, *kinda* hit the high note at the end of the first song but burst a vein and have no voice for the rest of the show! It means being able to sing through the entire show several times a week, through sickness, fatigue, and nerves.

Again, honesty is the best policy when it comes to setting your sights on the right role. Set yourself up for success, not failure, when it comes to your big audition.

Hear My Song

(*Songs for a New World*, 1995)

The most obvious source for audition material is the music from the show you're auditioning for.

A word to the wise: this method can easily backfire!

If you sing a song from the show, the director could decide that your interpretation of a role is not what he wants for this production. Also, sometimes directors explicitly state that they *don't* want to hear songs from the show they are going to do.

TIP: If you're not sure whether or not you should sing a particular selection, ask your teacher, director, choreographer, or anyone attached to the production and make a decision based on the opinions these people offer you.

If singing from the show isn't for you, start with musicals written in the same time period as the one you're auditioning for. As a general rule, it's best to pick music written within ten years of the show you're doing. However, the most important factor to consider when choosing audition material is the style of the music.

Most musical scores can be divided into one of two stylistic categories: legit and pop/rock.

Legit Musical Theater: This category includes pretty much any musical written before 1970. However, some newer musicals (e.g., *Parade, The Phantom of the Opera*, and *Ragtime*) also feature legit scores. The sound of this type of musical theater is closer to classical singing than to anything you would hear on the radio. Singers frequently use *vibrato*—vibration of the vocal cords that produces a pulsating pitch—in legit shows and rarely diverge from the notes that the composer has written for them to sing.

Pop/Rock: This includes newer shows that allow performers to sing more like popular recording artists you can hear on any radio station—hence the "pop" in the genre. Oftentimes, singers are allowed to alter the melody a composer has written in order to express the feelings of the character that sings them. This style makes greater use of the "straight tone," when a note is sung without vibrato.

Think *Rent, American Idiot, Spring Awakening, Hair*, etc.

After investigating the musical you're auditioning for, you should be able to decide what style the score is written in. Choose your audition material accordingly. In other words, it's probably not the best idea to sing Lady Gaga's "Poker Face" for your high school production of Gilbert and Sullivan's operetta *The Pirates of Penzance*.

Somebody Older

(*Steel Pier*, 1997)

Unless your school has lots of kids who were held back and a ton of child prodigies, chances are you will have to play roles that are older or younger than you are right now. But that's the greatest part of the theater: make-believe. The characters and situations in a musical show are larger than life, so why shouldn't you be able to play a crabby great-grandmother at twelve? Or a bratty preschooler at seventeen?

When taking on a role that's outside of your age range, it can be easy to fall into the trap of acting based on a stereotype of how you think a person that age would act. Instead, ask yourself what the character's reality is, then start to develop mannerisms based on what you find out.

Here are some questions to help get you started:

- How does the character talk? Is the character's voice higher or lower than my own? Does the character speak slowly or fly from idea to idea without pause?
- How does the character eat? Is it hard to chew? *How much* does the character eat? Is the character able to eat by himself, or does he require assistance?
- How does the character walk? Does he need outside assistance (e.g., another person, a walker, etc.)? Does the character have any noticeable disabilities?

The point of these questions is to help you discover the physical life of the character you're playing. Once that becomes second nature to you, it'll be easier to unlock the door into the character's soul.

Use What You Got

(*The Life*, 1990)

Now it's time to start figuring out what song you're going to sing for the big audition. Here's where all that research comes in handy!

The most important factor to consider when choosing a song is how you, the artist, connect to it.

TIP: Make sure you *like* the song you choose.

Under no circumstances should you ever choose a song that you don't enjoy performing. If you don't like singing the song, how can the people behind the table like watching you perform it?

Remember when you figured out your voice part in Chapter Two? The following is a list of good songs to sing—and NOT to sing—for your auditions, broken down by each voice type.

BASS

Sing This: "Wherever You Will Go" (The Calling), "I Walk the Line" (Johnny Cash), "Ol' Man River" (*Show Boat*)

Not This: "Never Say Never" (Justin Bieber), "Forget You" (Cee Lo Green), "I Could Have Danced All Night" (*My Fair Lady*)

BARITONE

Sing This: "Bubble Toes" (Jack Johnson), "(I've Had) The Time of My Life" (Bill Medley and Jennifer Warnes), "Make Them Hear You" (*Ragtime*)

Not This: "Can't Get Enough of Your Love, Babe" (Barry White), "Somebody to Love" (Queen), "Glitter and Be Gay" (*Candide*)

TENOR

Sing This: "Grenade" (Bruno Mars), "Don't Stop Believin'" (Journey), "Something's Coming" (*West Side Story*)

Not This: "Ain't No Sunshine" (Bill Withers), "Poker Face" (Lady Gaga), "Don't Cry For Me, Argentina" (*Evita*)

MEZZO-SOPRANO

Sing This: "Who Says" (Selena Gomez & The Scene), "Beautiful" (Christina Aguilera), "Maybe This Time" (*Cabaret*)

Not This: "Heartbreaker" (Pat Benatar), "Emotions" (Mariah Carey), "If I Were a Rich Man" (*Fiddler on the Roof*)

SOPRANO

Sing This: "You Belong with Me" (Taylor Swift), "I Will Always Love You" (Whitney Houston), "I Feel Pretty" (*West Side Story*)

Not This: "What the Hell" (Avril Lavigne), "Empire State of Mind" (Alicia Keys), "My Friends" (*Sweeney Todd*)

I Want to Make Magic

(*Fame on 42nd Street*, 1988)

It's time to address an important question you may have: What if I don't sing?

First, let's avoid making any statements about what you can't do and focus on what you *can*. Who knows if you can sing or not? Maybe you haven't had the opportunity to learn good vocal technique from a seasoned professional. Maybe you haven't been around music enough. The important thing is that you try, try, and try again.

Take a voice lesson. Stand at the piano and plunk out notes until you can match them. Listen to your favorite Broadway stars and try to imitate the way they sing. The most important thing about singing is *doing it*. Practice every day and pretty soon, you'll be amazed at what you have accomplished. And how good you sound.

Now, that's all fine and good, but what if you still don't feel comfortable singing in front of other people. This doesn't necessarily mean you can't be in a musical.

FACT: There are plenty of musicals that feature nonsinging roles or roles with very minimal singing. And the best part about these parts is the fact that they are, more often than not, the scene-stealers and crowd-pleasers (think Ermengarde in *Hello, Dolly!*, Pawnee Bill in *Annie Get Your Gun*, Madame Armfeldt in *A Little Night Music*, Lord Evelyn Oakleigh in *Anything Goes*, or Magenta in *The Rocky Horror Show*).

Research the show and find out if there are any of these type of roles in the show you're auditioning for. If you decide that you want a nonsinging track, you probably won't need to sing for the audition. Talk to your director or the people you'll be auditioning for and ask them what material you should prepare for your audition.

If this is the road you decide is right for you, be ready to impress! Because of the fact that there are fewer nonsinging tracks in a musical, you have to sell yourself as the only choice for the particular part you want. Otherwise, they may give it to a weak singer who auditions with a song anyway.

I Want to Go to Hollywood

(*Grand Hotel*, 1989)

Or maybe you're not interested in starring in a musical. Perhaps you want to join the glee club or show choir!

In many cases, the key to auditioning for one of these ensembles can be summed up in one word: cheese. Not only do you smile when you say the word, but glee clubs know how to sell camp, glitter, and jazz hands better than any other game in town. So, how do you get in with the cool kids?

Many glee clubs perform mash-ups of popular songs. So, turn on the radio and pick your favorite song that suits your voice and style. That's your audition piece!

Because popular music is not attached to specific characters, you can pretty much choose any song you like. In fact, one of the exciting parts of singing in a glee club is putting a new spin on popular music. The point is to sing well and sell, sell, sell.

Of course, you'll have to do your research when finding an audition song as well—starting with what kind of glee club your high school has. There are many pop/rock groups, sure, but there are also more traditional show choirs that sing mostly musical theater and standard repertoire (see Chapter Five).

Researching the group you'll be auditioning for—watching them perform, chatting with the musical director about his or her "vision" along with students who are already members of the group—will help provide useful information on what to prepare for the big audition day.

Most major music stores—both physical ones and online—will also sell sheet music for your favorite pop and rock artists. Be careful, though—you should have someone play the sheet music for you before your actual audition to make sure it's in the right key, especially if you're singing a song that is usually performed by someone with a different voice type than you. It's quite possible you may need the song *transposed* (which means having a piano player alter the key so it's more comfortable for you to sing). And never assume transposition can be done on the spot!

Along with glee clubs and shows choirs are a cappella groups, which perform without musical accompaniment. That means that you should prepare to sing *alone* for your audition—no sheet music or piano required. The only instruments these folks use are their voices. The people behind the table will want to hear if you can carry a tune and stay in the chosen key all while showing off your great personality.

TIP: Learn the song and drill it over and over so that you don't have to worry about the words or notes but can concentrate on giving a great performance.

Especially make sure you know your starting note—otherwise, the entire song might be thrown off. Even if the group doesn't use instruments, there will likely be a piano or a keyboard in the audition room. Don't be afraid to ask someone to pluck out your starting note. Or, even if there isn't a piano, the musical director should have a pitch pipe handy. Asking for help at the beginning of an audition doesn't mean you're unprepared—rather, it means you are conscientious and careful about giving a good performance.

Most glee clubs and show choirs feature lots of choreography, so it's important to show that you can move and dance in your audition. Up-tempo songs that allow you to rock out are usually the best. The people auditioning you want to see that you can let loose and have a good time. So start with your favorite song, add a dash of your own flavor and soul, and show them how it's *really* done!

CHAPTER FIVE
Show Choirs and Glee Clubs

If there is one thing that I have learned from my experience on *American Idol*, it is to always follow your heart and your intuition. It is usually always right. Take risks and just go for it because you never know where it may take you.

—EJAY DAY, TOP TEN FINALIST,
SEASON ONE OF *AMERICAN IDOL*

ost schools offer performance groups like show choir, vocal jazz, or a cappella—the perfect place if you dread the spotlight and simply want to be part of an ensemble. Here you'll find a familial spirit, a team bond, or heck—even a possible romance.

However, just because you're not in the spotlight doesn't mean performing in a group is easy. Quite the opposite—vocal ensembles provide their own set of challenges:

1. ***Singing:*** making music with your voice while projecting in front of an audience.
2. ***Dancing:*** choreographed steps performed as a group.
3. ***Blending:*** this involves great listening skills so you can recognize tonality in other voices.

This chapter will help you prepare for any one of these auditions so you know exactly what is expected of you in each scenario. Now, let's take a closer look at a few different types of singing groups that your school or community might offer.

Glee Club

Glee clubs originated in London, England, in 1787 and come from the English tradition of "part song," which is a form of choral music. "Part songs" were arranged for four voice parts divided into soprano, alto, tenor, and bass.

FACT: Glee club doesn't get its name from a musical mood that is sunny or peppy. Instead, glee refers to a type of choral piece from the late 1700s.

A "glee" was literally a type of song from the late baroque and early romantic periods in music, originally scored for three or four male voices and intended to be sung a cappella.

In 1858 the trend of glee reached America with a presence at Harvard University, and the club is still in existence! A traditional glee club features only males. Over time, large choral groups featuring a mix of men and women replaced the original notion of glee. Many colleges today simulate glee clubs in the form of a cappella groups or show choirs but often don't use "part songs" in their repertoire.

Another major difference between traditional glee club and show choir is the performance style and movement. Traditional glee clubs don't incorporate choreography and stand still while focusing on their musical blend, while in show choirs, costumes and choreography play a tremendous part in the presentation.

Does your school have a glee club? If so, find out if your troupe performs traditional glees or has simply retained the name and performs more modern choices.

Vocal Jazz

The Harlem Renaissance of the 1920s gave African Americans a cultural identity through music, art, and poetry. This musical era, along with the genres of Dixieland and Blues, overlapped with the jazz movement. Singers like Ma Rainey, Bessie Smith, Louis Armstrong, and Billie Holiday introduced vocals to jazz in a way that was traditionally expressed through trumpets, saxophones, and other instruments.

The end of the Swing era was followed by a new sound called Bebop, bringing Ella Fitzgerald to fame. Along with her silky tone and vocal dexterity, she is credited as one of the greatest scat singers of all time.

Scatting is defined as the use of "made-up" words—gibberish or syllables. Vocal scatting is usually accompanied by instruments, and shows off a singer's ability to improvise and inhabit the music. Unlike in a musical, for example, where the lyrics to a song tell a story, when you're scatting, you are meant to showcase your vocal chords as an instrument, and impress the audience with the awesome sounds you can produce.

5 SIMPLE WAYS TO SCAT

1. The first rule of vocal improvisation is that there are no rules. Scatting allows the singer to "let go" of the lyrics and be free with his/her voice. So really, you can do whatever you want!

2. Think of syllables as a language and be confident in your choices. Generally speaking, use a hard consonant followed by a vowel like "Bee Bop a Dee Doo" or "Doom Ba Doo Ba Da." These are guidelines but remember: no sound is wrong.

3. Know and utilize your musical scales (major, minor, chromatic, and pentatonic). Find your tonal center and master your interval relationships to guide your ear through chord progressions.

4. Ear training is key. You need to be able to produce sounds without looking at sheet music. Free your mind and listen to the musical accompaniment (whether it be piano, guitar, drums, or other voices) so you can be intuitive with your scatting.

5. Experiment with different tones, placements, and rhythms. Want to add some dark emotion? Add a "growl" to one of your notes. Feel like sounding light and pretty? Switch into your head voice. Overall, your goal is to use the nuances of your voice to present the music in a way that is completely "you" and has never been done before.

A vocal jazz ensemble can include eight to sixteen singers and musical backing of bass, guitar, drums, and piano. Due to complex and intricate arrangements, most ensembles do *not* use choreography. Depending on the group's size, there may be two voices assigned to each part—this is when your sharp sense of ear training comes into play!

TIP: Singing harmonies can be quite difficult. Before you audition for a vocal jazz ensemble, practice harmonizing with a friend who is auditioning for a different voice part. This is a great way to gain experience.

Show Choir

Around the same time as the birth of vocal jazz, show choirs developed. Show choir usually involves show tunes, lavish costumes, and precise choreography. While other vocal groups focus on stillness and blend, show choir creates stage pictures or full production numbers.

FACT: In 2009, the TV show *Glee* had 25 hits on the Top 100 *Billboard* charts, which is the most achieved by any artist since the Beatles in 1964. They even surpassed Elvis Presley, the King!

Show choir incorporates a range of costumes to fit a theme or theatrical concept. Anything from ball gowns, tuxedos, jeans and T-shirts, or flapper dresses have graced the show-choir stage. Show choir incorporates dramatic interpretation, facial expressions, and stage presence as another distinct quality. If you join show choir, be prepared to act!

Show choirs—much like sports teams—are known to participate in nationwide competitions.

TIP: A great resource is the documentary *Gleeful: The Real Show Choirs of America*. This film aired in the United Kingdom in 2010 and documented various high school experiences that paved the way for many Broadway and Hollywood stars. This film is a great guide for you to emulate choreography, vocal performances, and gain an overall understanding for show choirs of the highest standard.

A Cappella

A cappella singing refers to a sound produced without any instrumental backing.

While this form is traditionally part of the high school and competitive collegiate circuit, it has spilled over into mainstream music and reality television competitions. A cappella has even showed up in such Off-Broadway musicals as *Avenue X* and *In Transit*.

A cappella singing may be performed with the bare bones sound of no instrumental backing or it can utilize vocal percussion. This occurs when a vocalist emulates the sound of drums with his or her voice to add a pop/rock quality to the tone of the song.

FACT: Bobby McFerrin, ten-time Grammy Award winner, can swiftly switch between vocal registers and produce sounds with his voice that sound like they are coming from another instrument. And don't forget Justin Timberlake, who showed impressive beatbox moves with 'N Sync and in his solo music videos.

Joe Sofranko

The SoCal VoCals are a collegiate a cappella group from the University of Southern California that started in 1996. In 2008 and 2010 they had the honor of winning the grand prize at International Championship of A Cappella (ICCA). Joe Sofranko, former president of the SoCal VoCals, provides great insight for beatboxing:

Beatboxing is driven by three main factors: sound, rhythm, and tempo. When getting started:

1. You should constantly practice and play around with the sounds you can make in your mouth. Just explore!

2. Actually try to imitate the sounds of a drum set or the sounds you hear on the radio.

3. It's easy to fall out of tempo or rhythm when you're learning but you have to be strict with yourself about keeping consistent tempos.

You Can't Stop the Beat

(*Hairspray*, 2002)

The term *vocal percussion* is often interchanged with the term *beatboxing*.

Beatboxing requires the use of your voice, lips, tongue, and mouth as you simulate rhythmic instruments. Some artists use their hands cupped over their mouths as a mute to enhance or widen the variety of sounds produced.

TIP: You don't have to a great singer to be a great beatboxer. If you've always wanted to be part of an ensemble but don't think you have the singing chops, why not hone your rhythmic skills and become a vocal percussionist?

Five Easy Ways to Start Beatboxing

1. Listen to all kinds of music that incorporate a heavy bass and driving beat. These sounds are associated with Rap, Hip-Hop, Techno, House, or Rock.
2. Explore all the sounds you can make with your mouth. Purse your lips, gasp for air, or click your tongue.

3. Once you've built your own set of tones, try to emulate the sounds of a snare and drum set. Give this technique a whirl: say "boots" and "cats," starting off slowly and building to a faster pace. Soon enough you'll sound like a drum!
4. Don't be afraid to be silly—pick any letter of the alphabet and make a sound with it: "S" will have a hissing sound, while "K" might sound like a high hat drum. You'll never know until you try.
5. Incorporate beatboxing in fun ways like a talent show or creative English project. Find a group to join and perform in front of audiences!

Wanna Be Startin' Somethin'

(Michael Jackson, 1983)

If your school doesn't have an a cappella group, why not start one of your own?

First, contact the head of the music or theater department, or student government at your school—whomever you believe to be the authority in charge of forming this group. Elect yourself as the director or president and present the teacher with some kind of structured proposal.

Think about the following:

1. What skills are required for the participants?
2. How many people will the group hold?
3. How great of a commitment is required?
4. Where will you perform?
5. What costs are involved?

Once your proposal is solid, ask your teacher when you can have auditions and publicize. Hopefully you'll get a great turn out and then, based on the interest, you can develop your own rules.

When running rehearsals, a pitch pipe is essential because your starting pitch has to come from somewhere. A great way to find material that fits your group is to listen to all kinds of music—even genres you may not keep on your iPod. Step outside of your musical comfort zone—*then* you can be creative and take musical liberties by arranging your own version.

For new ideas, check out *Mouth Off*, a free, popular a cappella podcast. Rarb.org, the Recorded A Cappella Review Board, is a great site that reviews recorded a cappella albums and BOCA (the Best of A Cappella), the annual CD compilation of collegiate a cappella, is a fabulous learning tool. These various sources can help you find your footing as the group develops its sound. If obtaining sheet music for your arrangements becomes difficult, consider e-mailing various collegiate a cappella groups for help.

Once you've organized a group, check out the website Varsity Vocals (www.varsityvocals.com) to learn about competing. The organization holds regional competitions in search of finding top finalists. There's also the Contemporary A Cappella Society that give out awards, organizes events, and dedicates its mission to preserving the movement of modern day a cappella (www.casa.org).

Hopefully by now your imagination has run wild with options. So whether it means finding an audition or creating a group of your own, get out there and sing your heart out!

CHAPTER SIX

The Dance Call

Preparation is paramount. Soak up your craft and show business in general—see and read plays and movies; study acting and audition techniques; take voice lessons; read *Backstage* and *Variety*. Take advantage of the wealth of information available to help make you a well-informed and well-rounded actor.

—CRAIG BURNS, CSA/CASTING DIRECTOR/TELSEY + COMPANY (*WICKED, LEGALLY BLONDE, AND HAIRSPRAY*)

f you're aiming to land a spot in a musical or show choir, or want to perform a routine of your own for the talent show, you'll likely be asked to dance. The dance call can either be your best friend or your worst enemy, depending on how well you prepare.

POP QUIZ:

How Good of a Dancer Am I?

While you're dreaming big, it's time for a self-assessment.

A) Better than Sutton Foster, Beyoncé, and Bebe Neuwirth combined.

B) I dropped it like it was hot at every dance in middle school.

C) The Hokey Pokey required way too much hand-eye coordination.

D) Sutton who?

If you answered A or B you're off to a good start. If the honest truth is answer C or D, it's time to get dancing! And don't worry if you lack experience—it's never too late to start. Who knows? It may be love at first fouetté.

I Wanna Be a Rockette

(*Kicks: The Showgirl Musical*, 1984)

Start by honing your natural talent.

Feel free to croon into your hairbrush and dramatically pose in the mirror as a trial and error exercise. Ask yourself: *How does this feel and how do I look?*

The most important thing is to get comfortable in your own skin. Self-awareness is key when you're first getting the knack of things.

Eventually you'll have to dance on stage in front of people—but first, why not make up your own routine and share it with your family? You may even consider

DANCE FLASH!

Introductory Dance Terms

PIROUETTE [pir-oo-*et*]: to "whirl" or in this case a turn on one leg.
When Sarah was three, she did her first ***pirouette*** in ballet class.

PLIÉ [plee-ey]: "bent," in reference to your knees.
During warm-up exercises, the students ***plié*** and straighten their legs.

TENDU [tahn-*doo*]: "stretched," in reference to your legs.
When standing in first position, Carly's left leg remained straight while the right extended to ***tendu***.

In case you're wondering why these words sound foreign, it's because, well . . . they are.

They're French.

Although ballet evolved during the Italian Renaissance, King Louis the XIV of France loved ballet. King Louis formed the first official ballet school—known to the modern world as the Paris Opera Ballet. So even though he established the terminology in the 1600s, his practice stuck for centuries!

performing the routine at your school's talent show to get used to an unknown audience.

When you're ready, every school offers a range of extracurricular activities. If dance is an option, give it a try. Not only is class a great form of exercise—it can also be fun!

At the Ballet

(*A Chorus Line*, 1975)

You'll greatly benefit by picking up a dance history book and learning about some of the amazing dancers who preceded you. (*Song and Dance: The Musicals of Broadway* by Ted Sennett is a great place to start.) George Balanchine, Agnes de Mille, and Bob Fosse are among the legends who have changed the face of dance with their unique style and cutting-edge concepts.

All That Jazz

(*Chicago*, 1975)

In the late nineteenth century jazz evolved to make dancers seem more pedestrian—like everyday people walking on the street. It's a dance form that's supposed to be fun and allow you to let loose! (*Jazz* is often interchangeable with the term *Theater Dance*.)

Check out the DVD of *Fosse*, a Broadway musical tribute that features many of Bob Fosse's signature dance numbers. Classics like "Big Spender" (*Sweet Charity*), "Steam Heat" (*The Pajama Game*), and "Mein Herr" (*Cabaret*) reflect Fosse's wide range of characters, intricate choreography, and signature "knocked-knees" posture.

FACT: Bob Fosse's dancers were usually costumed in bowler hats, gloves, and fishnet tights to enhance the angular lines of the movement and the dancers' frames.

There's no reason to stop at ballet and jazz. Why not give tap a try? Or does another style tickle your fancy? Most dance studios have introduced modern and hip-hop on their rosters—try to immerse yourself in every form of dance available to you. Versatility will always benefit you in show biz!

And please don't think you have to quit gymnastics or ice skating to make time

DANCE FLASH!

More Dance Terms

BOX STEP: To make four points like a box with your feet by stepping across, back, side, and front.

Also known as a jazz square, the ***box step*** is commonly used in hoedowns.

GRAPE VINE: To cross back and forth with your feet.

Megan used the ***grape vine*** step to travel from stage left all the way to stage right.

BALL CHANGE: A change of weight distribution on the balls of the feet—a popular transitory step in many jazz dance routines.

When Jimmy does a kick, ***ball change***, he's sure to stay balanced and centered.

for dance. Your physical ability in any sport is a plus that will lend itself beautifully to dance. If you're a stunt master, you were born to perform in *Barnum*, *Tarzan*, Cirque du Soleil, and *Spider-Man: Turn off the Dark*.

My Strongest Suit

(*Aida*, 2000)

Let's forget about technique and rules for a minute and focus on personal flair.

That's right: I'm talking about the clothes!

Make sure to wear something formfitting that shows your lines and curves.

Girls, you can wear leotards, tights, jazz pants, or something snug to give you the freedom to move without feeling suffocated. Boys, feel free to wear leotards, too, or if you're uncomfortable getting all Spandex-y, dress like you're going to gym class in a formfitting T-shirt and shorts/pants. But whatever you do, avoid baggy clothes!

Lastly, and most importantly, you must have good shoes. Anything you wear for sports or Phys Ed should do the trick, but if you have to demonstrate a specific move for the choreographer, he may ask you to do so barefoot.

If you're serious about dance, you'll need to purchase the appropriate footwear. Capezio and Bloch are the retail leaders in dance apparel, so check out their

THE DANCE BAG

A professional dancer doesn't go anywhere without a dance bag. Inside, you should have the following:

1. Shoes. (Ballet, tap, jazz, character.)

2. Dance clothes. (Girls: leotard, bra, tights, shrug, skirt, shorts, leg warmers. Boys: leotard, formfitting T-shirt, shorts, pants.)

3. Street clothes. Nothing's worse than wearing sweaty clothes after the dance call. Travel-sized deodorant, and body powder are also handy, as well as hairpins, headbands, a small mirror, and a comb or brush, too!

4. Water. You'll need to hydrate your body so that you don't pass out. Also throw in a washcloth to absorb your sweat.

5. Snacks. Trail mix, granola bar, or a piece of fruit will give you the energy needed to dance your butt off.

websites to find a store near you. Highly recommended are the Capezio Stretch Jazz Ankle Boot (for jazz class), Capezio Fluid (for tap class), and Bloch's Pump Ballet Flat made from canvas.

TIP: It would be unwise to wear tap shoes to a ballet or jazz class because of the distracting sounds your feet will make. However, jazz and ballet shoes are built similarly and, therefore, can be worn interchangeably.

Moral of the story: If you *dress* the part from head to toe, you'll feel the part.

Go Into Your Dance

(*42nd Street*, 1980)

So it's the big day!

Before entering the audition room, make sure to give yourself a nice warm-up. Start with about five minutes of floor stretches to wake up your muscles. Hold each position for fifteen seconds.

1. Quadriceps: With one leg standing for support, bend the other at the knee and pull behind your body. The heel of your bent leg should (almost) touch your butt. Hold for fifteen seconds and repeat on the opposite side.
2. Hamstrings: Lie on floor with knees bent. Straighten one leg and slowly pull it toward your chest, clasping the thigh, calf, or ankle. Then switch legs.
3. Shoulder Strangle: Cross one arm horizontally over your chest, grasping it with either your hand or forearm, just above the elbow.
4. Chin to Chest Front: Place both hands behind your head, fingers interlocked, thumbs pointing down, elbows straight ahead. Slowly roll your head up and down ten times.
5. Hips and Butt: Sit on the floor with your right leg extended straight in front of you. Bend your left knee and cross it over your right leg, placing your left foot flat

on the floor next to the outside of your right knee. Put your right elbow on the outside of your left knee. Feel your whole torso twist away from your legs.

I Can't Stand Still

(*Footloose*, 1998)

When the choreographer is ready, he or she will introduce him/herself and explain a brief history of the piece about to be taught.

TIP: One way to nail the memorization, outside of dance class, is by watching music videos or theater clips.

Copy the moves, then time yourself to see how fast you can mimic the dancers. Try something challenging—like the choreography from Beyoncé's "Single Ladies"—and practice what it feels like to watch someone dance and repeat the movements.

Remember: Perfection isn't necessary—style, enthusiasm, and commitment to the steps give you major brownie points.

If you make a mistake, don't stop in the middle of the combination. Go until the end. This will show that you have a positive attitude and are a team player.

The documentary *Every Little Step* explores the audition process for the recent revival of *A Chorus Line*. It's an inspiring, real look at what it takes to be a professional dancer. And it's available on DVD.

I Wanna Be a Dancin' Man

(*The Belle of New York*, 1952)

Not every musical or show choir requires a lot of dance. The level of intricacy will vary from show to show and group to group.

TIP: Even in musicals with a lot of choreography, not every role requires equal levels of dancing. Before you audition, figure out which parts in the show best suit your talents so you can shine like the superstar you are.

With your great knowledge of dance vocabulary and the stories of great legends that came before you, there's no doubt you'll be successful.

A LIST OF SHOWS BROKEN DOWN BY LEVEL OF DANCE

Musicals with Little-to-No-Dance

Les Misérables, Into the Woods, Bat Boy: The Musical, Little Shop of Horrors, The Pirates of Penzance, The Sound of Music, Evita, Godspell, Jekyll and Hyde, Little Women, Man of La Mancha, The Mystery of Edwin Drood, Once Upon a Mattress, Once on This Island, Fiddler on the Roof, The Secret Garden, Ragtime, She Loves Me, Songs for a New World, Urinetown: The Musical

Middle of the Road

Bye Bye Birdie, Annie, The Drowsy Chaperone, Footloose, My Fair Lady, Grease, Gypsy, Hairspray, How to Succeed in Business Without Really Trying, Jesus Christ Superstar, Joseph and the Amazing Technicolor Dreamcoat, Kiss Me, Kate, Legally Blonde, Oliver, The Pajama Game, Pippin, Seussical, Show Boat, South Pacific, Spring Awakening

Highly Specialized Dance

A Chorus Line, West Side Story, Chicago, Cabaret, Carousel, Oklahoma!, Damn Yankees, Guys and Dolls, The Producers, Sweet Charity, The Wedding Singer

Tap Shows

Tap Dogs; Bring in 'da Noise, Bring in 'da Funk; 42nd Street; Anything Goes; Crazy for You; Thoroughly Modern Millie; White Christmas; Singin' in the Rain

USEFUL DANCE TERMS

ARABESQUE [a-ra-BESK]
A position of the body, in profile, supported on one leg, with the other leg extended behind and at right angles to it, the arms held in various harmonious positions creating the longest possible line from the fingertips to the toes.

CHAINE [shi-nay]
A turning movement in which the dancer executes a half turn on each foot.

CHASSÉ [sha-SAY]
A step in which one foot literally chases the other foot out of its position; done in a series.

FAN KICK
The body stays in place while one leg starts inward and kicks all the way around to its original position. These are often used in kick lines and Broadway-style routines.

JETÉ [zhuh-TAY]
Throwing step. A jump from one foot to the other in which the working leg is brushed into the air and appears to have been thrown.

LAYOUT
One leg is kicked up in the air, while the torso is leaned back into as dramatic an arch as possible. Head should be dropped, arms should also be extended backward.

PAS DE CHAT [pah duh shah]

A jump in which each foot in turn is raised to the opposite knee. The step owes its name to the likeness of the movement to a cat's leap.

PIVOT STEP

One foot steps in front of the other, and then the body pivots around into the original position.

ROND DE JAMBE [rawn duh zhahnb]

A circular movement of the leg.

RELEVÉ [ruhl-VAY]

A raising of the body on the points or demi-pointes of the feet.

SHUFFLE

A forward brush between your foot and the floor followed by a back brush to the front, side, or back, executed rapidly in a sixteenth-note rhythm.

TIME STEP

A repeatable combination that marks tempo. Time step can refer to an eight-measure movement placed at the beginning of a dance routine.

CHAPTER SEVEN
I'm Ready for My Close-Up

At the start of my career, I used to say: "I'd rather be lucky than good." I was half right. I should have said: "I'd rather be lucky *and* good." Everyone gets his or her shot, sometimes even more than once. It happens at the crossroad of opportunity (luck) and preparation (being good). The key is to stay in the game long enough for opportunity to strike, and to be the best in your field when it finally does.

—PAOLO MONTALBAN, (ABC/DISNEY'S *CINDERELLA*, BROADWAY'S *THE KING AND I*, AND *PACIFIC OVERTURES*)

Let's face it: Back in the eighties, Madonna was right. We *are* living in a material world—whether we like it or not.

When you walk into an audition, the first thing the creative team will see is what you look like. This doesn't mean you have to spend hundreds of dollars on clothes. Likely, everything you need is already in your closet.

Dressing the part is very specific to the individual. Wear an outfit that flatters you and accessories that speak to the character. Let's look at a practical example.

Say you're auditioning for *Rent* and you're a female going out for the role of Maureen. First you need to examine the basics of Maureen's character development.

WHO: Maureen Johnson

WHAT: Performance Artist. Recently dumped Mark. Now dating Joanne.

WHEN: 1989

WHERE: East Village, Manhattan (New York)

WHY: Maureen speaks out against injustice.

If you're not familiar with *Rent*, let your imagination run wild with these character traits. Go online and do some research, view clips from the show, or watch the movie. Look at pictures from the original Broadway production. That will help you begin to see what you might wear to your audition.

Now that you know a little something about Maureen's background, you're responsible for coming up with an audition outfit.

Why? 'Cause I'm a Guy!

(*I Love You, You're Perfect, Now Change*, 1996)

MACHO ALERT!

Boys, you also have to pay attention to what you're wearing. It's not just a female's responsibility to come dressed and ready to rock. Anything from jeans and

POP QUIZ:

Dress in the Style of Maureen Johnson

(Pick one of the following multiple-choice answers)

As Maureen Johnson, I would wear:

A) My Bat Mitzvah dress. What's the big deal? It still fits!

B) A cute blue sundress and strappy sandals.

C) Jeans, a funky top, and knee-high boots.

D) A bikini to show off your hot bod!

A isn't the best choice—Maureen Johnson would never wear a dress she wore a month ago, let alone a year ago. Plus something so formal would be inappropriate to audition for the role of a Bohemian hipster.

B is also problematic. Although the outfit could be appropriate in other auditions, it doesn't take into consideration the world in which this play is set. Maureen is outspoken and isn't a sweet, sundress-type of girl.

Although the bikini outfit fits Maureen's bold character in the context of the show, you need to respect those whom you're auditioning for and show up fully clothed.

Hopefully you understand why C is the most appropriate choice. Clothes inform a character, so as you study "Over the Moon" and "Take Me or Leave Me," your outfit will help you come alive and take on Maureen's essence.

a T-shirt to a button-down and slacks can be appropriate as long as you're mindful of the project.

Now it's your turn for a practice round!

You're auditioning for the role of Motel Kamzoil in *Fiddler on the Roof*. Motel is a poor Orthodox Jewish tailor living in Russia in 1905 and is madly in love with Tzeitel, the daughter of another poor family.

POP QUIZ:

Motel Kamzoil Attire

(Pick one of the following multiple-choice answers)

As Motel Kamzoil, it would be appropriate to wear:

A) An Ed Hardy T-shirt and shorts.

B) A tuxedo with black patent leather shoes.

C) All black attire, a Kippah (skull cap), a Jewish star, and Tzitzis (tassels worn by observant Jewish men).

D) Khaki slacks and a navy blue button-down, long-sleeved shirt.

Based on process of elimination, you picked A, right?! Just kidding. I give you more credit than that.

D is the best choice and C is thrown in there as a test. Your job is to *suggest* the role you're targeting without looking like you went out and purchased a costume. Although C may seem appropriate for the character (and you might wear something just like this in the actual production) it could read slightly desperate at an audition.

TIP: Try not to arrive looking like it's the first dress rehearsal. Instead, trust that the casting team will recognize your talent through an outfit that is suggestive of Motel's personality.

George Brescia

George Brescia, former vice president of Tommy Hilfiger, is a personal stylist and currently dresses individuals in the Broadway community. Some of his clientele include Victoria Clark (***Sister Act*, *The Light in the Piazza***), Taylor Hicks (***Grease***, winner of the fifth season of ***American Idol***), and Jonathan Groff (***Spring Awakening***, ***Hair***, and ***Glee***).

Here is some of his expertise about the best personal styling tips!

After years in the fashion industry, what is your impression of a great audition outfit? Where do you start?

GB: In the initial round you should look like your best self. Know the colors that look good on you. You always want to be illuminated.

What are some of the fashion DON'Ts you've observed?

GB: Guys often wear really worn-out, beat-down clothes and look disheveled. On girls, a bold printed top or dress can be distracting in the audition room, but then people may argue "I wore the tie-dye shirt and was remembered as 'tie-dye gal'" at the callback. Well, sure this situation may occur. But don't use your clothing as a gimmick. The casting team wants to focus on your face and you as an individual, instead of figuring out why your clothes are so "out there."

Is it always appropriate to look elegant, no matter the show or role?

GB: You will not impress a casting team by raiding your mom or aunt's closet. Instead you may read too mature, which takes away from the youthfulness. If you're auditioning for something period like Laurie in *Oklahoma!* or Clara in *The Light in Piazza*, consider a sundress and flats.

In a case like* American Idiot, *are street clothes acceptable?

GB: Wear what you wear in everyday life for characters that dress as such in the actual productions. If you're going in for something contemporary like *Mamma Mia!*, jeans and a T-shirt are expected.

If casting a show is like solving a mystery, is it true that casting directors want the actor to walk in with the solution?

GB: Yes! Casting directors want you to walk through the door and be "the one." Your clothes are the weaponry that go in your toolbox of success. When you're pulled together, it shows confidence and power. Rule of thumb is if you're wearing something that you would never wear in front of anyone else, the outfit should not make its first public appearance at an audition.

Can I work with the clothes I already have rather than go out and purchase an entirely new audition wardrobe?

GB: Absolutely! Go through your closet and find the articles that get you compliments regularly. It could be a simple T-shirt, but if you often hear "that looks so great on you," assess what it is that make people react this way. The cut? The color? The way it frames your figure? Be mindful of these details—they'll serve you tremendously.

For George Brescia's complete bio and testimonials, please visit www.georgebstyle.com.

A Little More Mascara

(*La Cage aux Folles*, 1983)

When it comes to makeup, you want to look like yourself but ramp up your features that are relevant for the character in your audition.

TIP: Audition makeup needs to be simple and clean. You can do a dramatic eye or rosy cheeks, but be aware that audition makeup is vastly different than stage makeup.

Stage makeup is designed to be big and flashy so that your features will read in a large theatrical venue with theatrical lighting and patrons in the balcony will still notice you. However, in a small audition studio, there may be harsh fluorescent lights and a mere fifteen feet of distance between you and the casting team.

Guys: In almost all cases, wearing makeup is not a great idea. If you don't wear it in life, no need to start for the purpose of an audition.

Let's say you're a dude auditioning for an original punk heavy metal musical. Just because you idolize Gene Simmons from Kiss doesn't mean you can walk into the room with a painted face. Instead, the casting team will wonder which planet you're from. If you come in made up like a clown, no one will take you seriously.

Instead, make sure you've showered, washed your face, styled your hair, and look as presentable as possible.

Auri Marcus

Girls: the root of good make-up is good skin. Makeup artist Auri Marcus offers her professional advice on audition makeup:

Your makeup should look replicable and effortlessly flawless. With minor exceptions, I always favor a natural look. In fact, most ***Spring Awakening*** and ***Mamma Mia!*** auditions require NO makeup to ensure that the actors look age appropriate.

Prep your skin with a primer so that you have a smooth canvas to work with and so that your makeup lasts all day (even through dance calls!). I'm a fan of liquid foundation—try HD foundation or apply your regular foundation with an HD brush. Mineral and/or powder foundations are great too! Most importantly, make sure that your foundation matches your skin, and that it doesn't look like you're wearing foundation.

If your skin is near perfect, I recommend a light dusting of powder to even out the skin tone, and concealer for imperfections and under-eye circles. I love thick lashes, a barely noticeable amount of eyeliner (wiggled into the lashline), flushed cheeks, and glossy lips. It sounds like a lot, but all of this can be achieved in five minutes or less.

These tips are meant to be a guide but please keep in mind that most importantly, you should look like YOU!

GOING GREEN

"You don't prepare for Elphaba—you become her.

The lead role in *Wicked* is musical theater's equivalent of a triathlon. The show is nearly three hours long. In that time Elphaba navigates the dark halls of high school, casts spells, defies gravity, and belts some of the toughest songs ever written for the stage.

Oh, yeah—for the second act she wears a thirty-pound dress!

I would start the "greening" process alone, painting my hands, the cracks of my knuckles and in between my fingers. My fingernails were always painted green. My real transformation, however, did not begin until thirty minutes before curtain—that's when my hair and makeup artists arrived in my dressing room to work their magic.

The hair and makeup process is extensive, but the timing is so specific, so meticulous, that all of the makeup, the pin curls and wigging, takes only twenty to twenty-five minutes. Surprisingly, the process was very peaceful. I would sit in my swivel chair, and get into character—let go of the day I had, and focus on the journey I was about to take as Elphaba.

Wicked is a fairy tale, but for the duration of the show, Elphaba is real. Her face, neck, chest, even her hairline are visible. The audience must believe in her journey, which starts with her identity: Elphaba is a witch. It's quite a challenge for the make artist. My hair stylist is equally integral for my transformation.

She adds another layer of texture, crafting a unique look for one of Broadway's most memorable characters.

During the show, almost every time I was offstage, there was some sort of green touch-up. At intermission, Elphaba ages, becoming darker and more glamorous with shading, eyelashes, and a more sophisticated hairdo.

After the show, getting the green off was a process in itself. Armed with a makeup remover towel, I would start with my lips, then eyes, then jump in the shower and go to war. That paint is water-based, but is still a challenge to get off. Dr. Bronner's peppermint soap is an Elphaba favorite. I eventually came to terms with the fact that I wasn't gonna get it all off, and since it was all going on again the next day, I learned to live with it, find the humor in it, and really appreciate the experience of becoming Elphaba."

Carrie Manolakos has performed the role of Elphaba across the United States on tour with *Wicked*. She has also appeared on Broadway as Sophie Sheridan in *Mamma Mia!* Visit her at www.carriemanolakos.com.

HAIR

(*Hair*, 1967, Off-Broadway)

Every time you head out to the movies with your crew or prep for the annual Spring Fling, your hair is just as much a part of the look as the rest of your outfit.

The same applies in an audition.

Style your natural hair appropriately to the time period of the show. If you're auditioning for *The Wedding Singer*, channel your inner Cyndi Lauper and display your fabulously big and poofy eighties hair. If the character is more uptight or formal, like Marian the librarian in *The Music Man*, a pulled back updo or a tight bun will be fitting.

Always travel to auditions with reinforcements. Have a combination of bobby pins, gel, styling products, and a brush or comb in your bag. Weather and the temperature of the audition room are other factors that can affect your 'do, so *don't* forget the hairspray.

Guys and gals with short hair—your options are more limited. But have no fear! Instead, focus on the other elements of your physical presentation to help the casting team visualize you in their production. Guys, go to a barber and get a trim. Girls with short hair—make sure it's stylized and intriguing. People love bobs—look at the 1920s!

Giving your hair and makeup some well-deserved attention will pay off—trust me. After all, looking your best only helps your star to shine a little brighter.

You Gotta Get a Gimmick

(*Gypsy*, 1959)

Now that you look your best, what else can you do that will make your audition memorable?

There's a famous story about how Barbra Streisand once walked into an audition chewing gum and before starting her monologue, she stuck the piece of gum underneath the stool she was sitting on. Once she finished the audition, the people behind the table got up and checked underneath the stool to see where the gum was. Alas, there was no gum to be found. It had all been a gimmick. She wanted to be in character from the minute she walked through the door until the minute she left the room. And she landed the role!

If this sounds up your alley, try coming up with something equally inventive to make your audition go from ordinary to extraordinary. What about an interesting accessory that you can make use of in the audition—a fancy brooch or watch? Or styling your hair a different way so that you can incorporate it into your performance?

TIP: Don't come in complete costume to the audition. Kevin Kline showed up to an audition for *On the Twentieth Century* in a cape and period-specific suit and happened to get the part. But you're not Kevin Kline. Yet.

Whatever device you decide to feature, make sure that it does not become the focal point of your audition. Never lose sight of what the song is actually about in order to sell a cheap gag or trick. While gimmicks can be handy, they are not ultimately what you're trying to showcase.

You're trying to showcase *you*.

Warming Up

Do at least one thing every day to improve your skills and/or opportunities. For instance, take a dance class, vocalize, see a show, work on a song/monologue. Read! Get close to folks who share the same interests. And don't say you're right. SHOW you're right. After all, it's Acting.

—DAPHNE RUBIN-VEGA, TWO-TIME TONY AWARD NOMINEE AND ORIGINAL MIMI IN *RENT*

A runner needs to fuel his body before a race.

A writer needs to think before she puts words down on a piece of paper.

And you—a performer—need to prep before your big audition.

Gettin' Ready Rag

(*Ragtime*, 1996)

Let's say you're auditioning for your school's talent show and playing one of your original songs on the piano.

Your preparation needs to start the night before. Eat a good meal (high in protein, like grilled chicken or red meat) and get a good night's sleep. Don't stay up all night practicing—you'll only be tired the next day. Rest up! Your body will thank you later.

The morning of your audition, wake up early. You don't want to oversleep and then be rushing around. It will be stressful, and you may not give your best audition as a result.

TIP: Set yourself up for success. Eat a healthy breakfast (oatmeal with fresh fruit is a great choice, or eggs with the yolk for a good protein source).

Showering and getting dressed should be obvious, but what's very easy to forget is *warming up*. This refers both to your body and your voice.

If you're a dancer, you'll be used to stretching before you dance. The same applies for any audition—you need to move around and get the blood flowing to help your body relax, and you need to get your singing voice ready.

Why? You don't want to appear stiff or rigid while you're performing. Also, you don't want the first time you'll be singing to be in front of the director or musical director. Your voice is an instrument—just like you'd tune your guitar to make sure everything is in working order, you need to do the exact same thing for your voice.

The Five-Minute Warm-Up

Before you sing, you should always warm up (aka vocalize).

In voice lessons, sometimes you spend an entire half hour warming up before you even sing a song. Before a show, the music director will warm you up—but at auditions, you don't often have the luxury of a piano or even a room you can go inside, close the door, and belt your face off.

Here are five easy exercises you can do to get ready when you're in less than ideal singing circumstances. Each one should take about a minute, and they should be done in order.

1. STRETCH IT OUT

Singing isn't just about your voice. It's about your entire body. Before you even attempt to sing, make sure you've stretched. Start by bending over and reaching to the floor. Try and touch your toes, but if you can't, simply let your arms hang. Swing them back and forth or hold them still—it doesn't matter. The important thing is to be loose and tension-free.

Once you've done this, stand back up. This time, when you bend over, take a deep breath and hold it. When you stand, let the air out while panting like a dog. This is going to get your breath flowing and your diaphragm contracting. Repeat two or three more times.

2. ROLLING ALONG

Neck rolls? Check. Shoulder rolls? Check. Afterward, massage your fingers into your sinuses and the pockets of your cheeks, opening them up. Massage your neck, and—gently—your throat, including your voice box (also known as your larynx, which is located at the top of your windpipe).

3. LIP TRILLS

A lip trill is when you press your lips together and vibrate them to make a buzzing sound. They help to warm up the vocal chords gently before singing.

Do a series of lip trills going up and down a scale. Going from low to very high is important, and these trills should be light and airy—not forced. If you have trouble doing a lip trill, hold your fingers on either side of your mouth and push up, as if you are trying to make yourself smile. This will help until you can do them all on your own.

4. START WITH SOMETHING NASAL

A lot of times, it's easy for your voice to get "caught"—when you sing, it will sound like someone shoved a trumpet mute down your throat. The first vocal exercises you want to do should be very nasal. Try the word "nyang" or "mee-ah." This will help.

Then, start with your vowels. Do a few scales going up and down with the word "ma" and then "me." Don't worry about how high or low you're singing; concentrate on the sounds you're creating and getting your vocal chords ready.

5. REACH FOR THE SKY

The last quick warm-up should take your voice as high as you will need to be singing in the audition. A good tip is to sing a few notes higher than you will need to and make sure the top of your voice is warm and ready to go. If you've already hit even higher notes in warm-up than when you'll be performing, it will lessen your anxiety.

Be careful not to blow your voice out. Don't sing harder or louder than necessary. A few scales will do. The last thing you want is to sing yourself sick so that, when it actually matters, your voice is too tired to perform.

Tea for Two

(No, No, Nanette, 1925)

Most people prefer to eat a few hours before their audition—that way their bodies have time to digest the food, and you won't feel bloated or "full" when you walk in to sing your song, dance your dance, or play your instrument.

But many folks will also drink fluids right up until their audition—they may even bring a water bottle *into* the audition room!

It's important to stay hydrated, but drinking gallons of water won't magically improve your singing voice. It's a good idea to have a water bottle nearby, but don't use it as a crutch. Focus on preparing your audition, relaxing mentally (and physically!), and gearing up to perform like the superstar you are.

Many people believe drinking hot tea is a magic cure for your sore throat, but before you start sipping away, let's clear up a few myths about what you *should* and should *not* drink before an audition.

While hot drinks can prove quite effective in soothing a sore throat, not just any drink will do. Drinks with high levels of acidity and caffeine can actually damage your vocal chords, and *certainly* should not be consumed before one has to sing.

Coffee: Bad. Coffee by nature is bitter, strong, and drying. Plus, the caffeine will make it more difficult to sing and speak on stage. This also goes for any and all energy drinks (e.g., Red Bull).

Tea: While herbal teas are good for you, some teas have just as high caffeine/acid levels as coffee. It's easy to fool yourself into thinking you are drinking something good for your voice when, in fact, it can actually be detrimental. Stay away from dark teas like English Breakfast, and don't let the tea bag steep for too long. Generally speaking, chamomile is the way to go.

Milk: A big no-no. The last thing you want to drink before you perform is dairy—it will create phlegm that will make your voice scratchy, heavy, and thick. Instead of singing like a bird, you'll be hocking up a loogie the entire show.

Apple Juice: The singer's secret. Apple juice is sweet and coats the throat; it can often be a quick fix to drink right before a show. Too much of a good thing can easily be bad, however, so drink with caution.

Water: The staple. You'll never go wrong with water, but it's not magic. Drinking ten bottles isn't any more effective than drinking a few sips. Room-temperature water is much better for your voice than a bottle right out of the fridge. Your body will spend less energy processing it, and it's less of a "shock" to your vocal chords.

HOMEMADE STEAMER

If you're caught without a steamer, never fear—you can make your own in three easy steps.

1. Fill a large pot with hot water. You can do this in any sink (kitchen, bathroom).

2. Take a towel from the bathroom and hold it over your head, or have someone hold it for you.

3. Lower your head above the water and hold out the towel, which will trap the rising steam from going into the air and keep it concentrated around your face. Take a few deep breaths through your nose, then raise your head from the pot.

Almost immediately, you will notice that your sinuses are opening up, and you'll be able breath. Repeat as necessary.

Adelaide's Lament

(*Guys and Dolls*, 1950)

Let's say you wake up and feel terrible. Nothing is worse than compromising your health—take your temperature and evaluate whether you're well enough to get out of bed and audition. That's a decision that only *you* can make. If you do cancel, you'll be forgiven—just make sure to have someone inform the director or musical director that you won't be making it.

If you decide that you're sick, but not too sick to miss the audition, there are a few things you can do to feel better quickly.

Warm It Up: If your throat is sore, or you have a stuffy nose, take a hot shower. The steam will help to clear your sinuses and soothe your throat. You can also sleep with a humidifier, use a neti pot or a steamer that you purchased at the drugstore, or even create a makeshift steamer at home.

These days, getting sick really isn't the end of the world. There are nose and throat sprays, and tons of over-the-counter goodies to help you feel better so you can give a great audition.

TIP: A good cough drop is your friend.

If your throat is sore, your instinct might be to use a numbing spray or cough drop. You may feel better in the short run, but this could definitely work against your audition. With your throat numb, you won't be able to feel it—which means you won't know your own limitations.

You may need to make some adjustments in what you're performing. Maybe you won't sing the song with the huge belt at the end—instead, you'll choose something quieter and more introspective. But if your throat is numb, you might think you can sing like you normally can . . . and then you create the potential to crack in the audition room.

Better to use soothing drops with honey or lemon. Ricola is always a good choice, and Fisherman's Friend is a strong cough drop that will also work to open up your sinuses.

And if you're craving something warm to drink, try organic Throat Coat tea, which is made with licorice root to help soothe your aching throat.

Just remember: there's a fine line between rising to the occasion and not letting a cold get you down, and recognizing when you truly are too ill to perform. Talk to your parents and teachers to figure out which side of that line you fall on. There will always be more auditions, but there's only one you—so take care of yourself!

CHAPTER NINE
How to Be Professional
ROLL

The best advice I can give to an aspiring superstar is to showcase your strengths and know yourself as an artist, person, and performer. The best thing you can give in a room is yourself. It's about bringing yourself to the character instead of bringing the character to you. The most common misconception in this business is that you have to become something or fit a mold. The business is changing constantly and there is no longer a formula for success. People are creating their own success and platforms every day. Know yourself, celebrate yourself, and bring yourself to the table and you cannot go wrong.

—JEN NAMOFF, SOFFER/NAMOFF ENTERTAINMENT
AND PRODUCER OF THE 2011 TONY AWARD–WINNING REVIVAL OF
HOW TO SUCCEED IN BUSINESS WITHOUT REALLY TRYING

A wise man named Shakespeare once wrote "All the world's a stage and all the men and women merely players. They have their exits and their entrances and one man in his time plays many parts."

Life is about role-playing. For instance, you probably don't act the same way with your BFF that you would with your parents, right? In this chapter, you'll learn about self-assessment and actions that can enhance your presentation to conquer the audition!

This Is the Moment

(Jekyll & Hyde, 1997)

Entering the audition room is all about being yourself.

Keep your chest up and your chin high, exuding confidence. As you deliver your piece—whether it's a monologue or a song—project your voice. What's the point of acting if no one can hear you? As Mama Rose once said, "Sing out, Louise!"

When you audition, view the room as your stage. You may be lucky enough to audition on the *actual* stage where your performance will take place. But if you're in a studio or a classroom, despite the scaled-down nature of the room, imagine the space as your arena. The energy and charisma you bring to your audition will help the director see your potential for a full performance.

You may already have a personal relationship with the person you're auditioning for. If so, there's no need to get formal. Instead, have a few brief words or an exchange of "hellos." This breaks the tension in the room and will make you feel at ease. And if the director, musical director, or choreographer doesn't already know you, it's important for them to see your natural charm.

So how does one break the ice? You can never go wrong with the following:

1. "Hello, how are you?"
2. "Hi, how's your day going?"

3. "Hello, my name is _____ and I will be presenting ______."

Whatever you choose, make sure to clearly articulate your introduction. First impressions are everything!

Charles Gilbert

Charles Gilbert, director of the Ira Brind School of Theater at the University of the Arts, offers an insider's scoop:

It's important to remember that the people you'll be auditioning for are not your enemies. Believe it or not, they are looking forward to meeting you. Of course, the logistics of auditioning mean that often a number of candidates get crammed into a short period of time, and schedule pressure and fatigue can make the people behind the table a little grumpy. However, after years of auditioning students for the University of the Arts, I still look forward to meeting talented young actors and theater artists.

I Can't Do It Alone

(*Chicago*, 1975)

Accompanist: One who follows you in a musical way, by providing the piano instrumental part underneath your performance.

In a sense, the accompanist is your musical backbone. Once you establish a tempo and indicate your particular "audition cut," (more on this in a sec!) you rely on each other to stay in sync.

After you introduce yourself to the director, walk over to the pianist and briefly discuss your musical selection. More than likely you'll sing an "audition cut," which refers to a range of 16–32 musical bars. This selection is something you must pre-determine either with a friend or vocal coach, and it should demonstrate your vocal range and acting chops. Indicate on the sheet music where the accompanist should start and finish and if there's a key change or tempo shift so you're on the same page (literally and figuratively!).

TIP: The best way to figure out how many bars of music you should sing is to count them out. A bar will be separated by a vertical line in the music staff.

Martin Landry

Martin Landry, pianist/conductor of Off-Broadway's *Dear Edwina* and professional audition accompanist provides great tips for auditioning:

No matter how well-known your audition song is, never assume the accompanist knows it. Make sure your music is in a binder, with easy-to-turn pages. If you put your music in plastic sleeves, make sure they're not too reflective, as it can be difficult to read in certain lighting.

Don't use loose pages. Nine times out of ten, they will fall off the piano during your audition. With photocopied music, make sure the piano part is completely intact. Check the bottom of each page to make sure every note in the bass clef is showing.

Show the accompanist your tempo by singing a line of the song. You can also pat your leg, or tap your foot or the piano to help establish your speed.

If the accompanist plays a wrong note or two during your audition, don't get too upset. Mistakes happen—it's up to you to do your best *no matter what*. Be careful not to roll your eyes or behave in an immature fashion. Even if you are slightly displeased with the audition, leave the room with a smile, take a deep breath on your way out, and simply let it go.

On My Own

(*Les Misérables*, 1985)

There may come a time when you will fly solo without a pianist. You may sing a cappella for a show choir audition, or perhaps you've brought in your guitar to audition for the school talent show and no piano is necessary.

In these cases, you're not responsible to share sheet music with anyone else. Just like the previously mentioned auditions, your entrance must be strong. Memorize your selection or read off sheet music, but don't get lost in the page. Make sure your body language is open and present, and that your gaze is out—not at the floor.

SHOW CHOIR SCENARIO: The director needs to hear your tone without any musical backing. Feel free to move your body, tap your foot, or riff on notes to express yourself.

TALENT SHOW SCENARIO: Your voice and your instrument are the whole package. In this case, feel free to rock on with your guitar or jam out on the piano—engage just like you would at any concert.

Don't forget: performing live music is all about connecting with your audience and making them feel something special inside!

Here's Where I Stand

(*Camp*, 2003)

Now that stride and posture have been addressed, you may wonder: where exactly do I plant myself in the room?

Some directors may establish a place on the floor for the "auditionee" to stand. However, it's equally as common for directors to leave that up to you. In general, somewhere central in the room is always a strong choice.

PLACES YOU SHOULDN'T STAND

- Huddled in a corner, even if you're singing "In My Own Little Corner" from *Cinderella*. The creative team needs to see your face; don't distance yourself too much.
- Directly hugging the piano. Your body and voice need to be free—clinging to the piano will make you tense, downplaying your full power.
- One inch in front of the audition table. The director wants to see you but doesn't need to smell the tuna you had for lunch.

The Spark of Creation

(*Children Of Eden*, 1991)

By now, you understand that being a superstar isn't simply about having a great voice or being an amazing dancer. It requires acting ability and imagination, and most of all—confidence. One fantastic way to give the audition team a sense of your personality is to interpret a song in a creative fashion.

In certain cases it's important to sing a song as written and act it sincerely. Other times, it could be fun to show that you don't take yourself too seriously and know how to put your own spin on the song. This can include changing around lyrics by writing your own while keeping the melody intact. You might also use a funny prop that raises the stakes of the original intention or incorporates a new joke that wasn't there before.

CREATIVITY COUNTS

Sometimes, thinking outside of the box really works.

Natalie Weiss (Broadway's *Everyday Rapture*) once sang the pop song "Alone" by Heart in a *Xanadu* audition to a chocolate bar.

Actress Mara Jill Herman once sang "Lady Marmalade" in a *Jesus Christ Superstar* callback and changed the lyrics to: "He met Magdalene down in old Jerusalem, strutting her stuff on the street, she said 'Hello, Hey Jesus, you wanna give it a go?'"

Being a performing artist is about taking risks. It may seem strange or "wrong" to deliver the material in a way that is shocking, ironic, or campy unless you've been directed that way, but bold choices can serve you tremendously.

I'm Coming Out of My Shell

(*A Year with Frog and Toad*, 2002)

It's to be expected that first-timers may deal with some stage fright.

5 WAYS TO COPE WITH BEING NERVOUS

1. Close your eyes and take deep breaths.
2. Attempt some relaxation techniques like meditation or yoga.

3. Go for a walk to clear your mind.
4. Warm up your mouth and voice—by putting your attention on a specific activity, this makes your mind wander less and gives you a focus.
5. Remind yourself that you are a *superstar* and that the person you're auditioning for is excited to meet you!

What You Want

(*Legally Blonde*, 2007)

When it's time to deliver a song or monologue, your hands should be at ease by your sides. If you naturally move them around that's perfectly acceptable, too. Just avoid the trap of illustrating, which makes the performance seem amateur and silly. Illustrating refers to a matched gesture with almost every word. Directors don't want to mistake your audition for a round of charades!

For example, illustrating the song "When I Fall in Love," made famous by Doris Day, Celine Dion, and others, might look like this:

Pointing to yourself on the word "I"

Falling down to the ground on the word "fall"

Pointing to your heart on the word "love"

This kind of acting doesn't leave anything to the imagination of the audience. Instead, focus on sharing your story with facial expression and natural body language.

Where you look when you audition is a tricky one. Some casting people don't mind if you look right at them. Others would say they don't mind when you sing to a spot on the wall, right above their heads, or on a similar eye level. You certainly don't want to place your focus on the ground or up to the ceiling because you will appear nervous and disconnected from your performance.

TIP: Even when you're singing a solo or reciting a monologue, you must have an imaginary scene partner with you. Make sure you know to whom you're singing, or if you're alone onstage (i.e., Billy Bigelow in "Soliloquy" from *Carousel*), what you're singing about. It is important to look at the lyrics and understand the meaning of what you are saying. Only then can you relate "emotion" to the people you are auditioning for.

Always Look on the Bright Side of Life

(*Monty Python's Spamalot*, 2005)

Everyone dreads it. It makes you sweat. But the truth is, it's bound to occur. At some point during an audition, you *will* mess up. It happens to the best of us.

A mistake in an audition (or even in a live performance) can be okay as long as you know how to recover. The old saying "the show must go on" is particularly true in the case of an unexpected blunder.

Scenario #1: You're singing and your voice cracks. No big! Just move on as if it didn't happen at all. *Don't* have a meltdown or throw a hissy fit—this will only bring more attention to the mistake. A crack might seem like a big deal to you, but your audience will forgive a two-second distraction if the overall performance is solid.

Scenario #2: You're singing and you forget a word. No worries! If you fudge a lyric and can't think of anything to say, it's not the end of the world if you start humming. Chances are your mind went elsewhere for a split second and the lyrics will come back to you. If you are completely blank and absolutely have to, politely ask the pianist and the director if you can start again. Like restarting a computer, you may need to simply reboot your system to give a memorable audition of which you feel proud.

The most important thing? When you *do* have these unpredictable moments in your audition, stay composed. This is a chance for your auditioner to see your natural personality come through. Maybe they'll commend you because you can easily laugh off a small mistake. They don't want to discover, however, that you have a bad attitude and get all heated over something minor. So no matter what happens, it's not the end of the world. After all, auditions should be fun!

DON'T: Flip out if you say the wrong words/forget some entirely. No one is following the script or score to judge if you're word perfect.

DO: Practice. A useful technique in understanding the story of your song is to recite the lyrics like a monologue. This will ensure that you know what thoughts you're communicating and make your performance stellar.

These are just a few simple ways to enter your audition with the right frame of mind. Practicing these good habits now will ultimately lead to great character research and preparation when the rehearsal process begins.

CHAPTER TEN
Dealing with
Disappointment

To any future superstars considering getting into the entertainment industry, I would say you have to be thick-skinned and determined. As thrilling as it is to sing and act in amazing songs and stories, meet incredibly talented people, or hear an audience give a standing ovation, you have to able to deal with a fair amount of rejection and lows. [You] have to be patient, and be able to run with the "highs" as well as the "lows." To all the future superstars out there, learning this would be my biggest piece of advice.

—JOSHUA HENRY,
TONY NOMINEE FOR *THE SCOTTSBORO BOYS*

isappointment is a part of life no matter what you do, but especially when it comes to performing.

You must have a strong stomach. And with some pointers, you can channel your feelings of disappointment into something productive.

Don't Cry for Me, Argentina

(*Evita*, 1978)

If you didn't land the part you wanted, no matter how upset you are, take it like a champ. This advice is the same if you auditioned for your school talent show and didn't make the cut, the show choir, or any audition, really.

Sometimes you'll win, and sometimes you'll lose. That's life. The most important thing is how you deal with it.

Not getting the musical opportunity you wanted isn't the end of the world, but it can certainly *feel* like it. Acknowledging that you're upset is good and, more importantly, healthy. If you need to cry, then cry. If you need to bang your fist against the wall, then bang your fist against the wall—but don't break a nail. Or a finger. Allow yourself to feel exactly what you are feeling—anger, sadness, insecurity, whatever—but when you leave that bathroom stall, leave those feelings there, too.

At least until you get home.

Put on a Happy Face

(*Bye Bye Birdie*, 1960)

It's okay to share your disappointment with your friends, but you don't want to become known as a Downer. After all, a smile and a quick "congratulations!" means a lot. If you run into someone in the hall who got cast in the show, reach out to him or her.

BROADWAY GOSSIP:

A Trio of Leading Ladies

Before the Tony Award–winning musical *Thoroughly Modern Millie* found its star, Sutton Foster, the production went through two other leading ladies.

First was Kristin Chenoweth, who played the role in the original workshop and bowed out at the chance for her own television sitcom, *Kristin*.

Second was Erin Dilly, who starred in the role at the La Jolla Playhouse in 2000. Dilly, however, was unexpectedly replaced during previews by her very own understudy, Sutton Foster, who had auditioned for the role of Millie but was placed in the ensemble instead.

Foster then went on to star as the lead in the new Broadway musical receiving numerous accolades including the ultimate prize: the 2002 Tony Award for Best Leading Actress in a Musical.

TIP: If you don't have anything nice to say, make something up.

If you go out of your way to avoid people in the show, it will look suspicious. It's better to pretend you're happy for them—even if you're not—because eventually these are people you will want on your side. If you alienate yourself from the rest of the cast with your sour puss, you might be excluded from fun parties and rehearsal breaks.

Besides, today's chorus member is tomorrow's star. You never know who is going to leave for the summer as a caterpillar and return to school as a butterfly.

FACT: There is always room to grow and improve.

Didn't grab the solo you wanted in show choir? That's okay—work on perfecting your craft so that the next time you audition, you'll be even better.

There's a reason that people say "practice makes perfect"—because it's true. It's very rare that anyone, no matter how talented you are, gets every part, every solo, all the time. Rejection is part of what it means to be a superstar. And knowing what it feels like *not* to get something you want will make the times when you do get the solo, the part, or the opportunity of your dreams mean that much more.

The Nice Way Is the Right Way

Here are some helpful tips on how to translate how you feel into something appropriate to *say*:

It's important to take the high road and not say anything you might regret. That way, when you're the one who gets the lead role, people are happy for you.

HOW YOU FEEL	WHAT TO SAY
Looking at you makes me want to throw up all over myself, or rather, all over you.	You look so good today.
The fact that you got that part instead of me makes me think the entire world is unfair and out to get me.	Congrats on the part! You *so* deserved it.
Is the director deaf? You can't sing at all, and you couldn't act your way out of a box if your life depended on it!	I just *knew* your talent would finally be recognized.

~~There are no small parts, only small actors.~~ Sometimes there are small parts. Deal with It!

It's just the way it is. Not everyone can be the lead. Not everyone wants to be, either, and sometimes the best—and most rewarding—roles are the smaller ones. Maybe you're not onstage the entire show, but supporting roles are usually much juicier, with the funniest lines or most dramatic moments.

Once you move past your initial disappointment, you will realize that it's wonderful to simply be part of a show in the first place—even if that means not having a single solo or speaking line.

You might not get the lead solo in your show choir, but you still get to be part of the group, making music and having fun. Sometimes that's just as important (if not more important) than being the star.

PLUS: *The pressure is off*

When the show isn't resting on your shoulders, there's a lot more time to relax and enjoy the creative process. Bond with your fellow performers. Watch the show from the sidelines and appreciate it for the work of art that it is.

PLUS: *Getting experience*

Being in the ensemble can be extremely rewarding in the sense that a) you're an essential part of the show and b) it gives you the opportunity to observe older and more experienced actors, studying how they approach their craft so that when your times comes, you can make the most of it. Maybe you're not ready for the big solo in your show choir this year . . . but that doesn't mean you won't be next year.

PLUS: *Putting in your time*

Everyone has to pay his or her dues—even professionals. A year or two in the ensemble won't go unrecognized: the director will see your passion and enthusiasm, and remember how hard working you are when it comes time that you're a senior.

Karma Chameleon

(*Taboo*, 2002)

Everyone loves a go-getter—someone who makes opportunities *happen*.

TIP: Be proactive.

If you find that you're sitting around during rehearsal with lots of free time on your hands, offer to help the director. Does he need someone to help take notes or make photocopies? Would you be able to understudy one of the larger roles just for the experience? Can you help some of the other singers with their harmonies?

You never know until you ask. But you shouldn't offer your help just because you want something. Do it because you're eager to learn and make the show as good as it can possibly be.

If you send good vibes out into the world, they will come back to you, in some form or another. This is what we call karma.

CHAPTER ELEVEN
Be Creative!

For me, acting has always been about striving to create something that is truthful, interesting, and new. In every aspect of my acting, whether that's at an audition, on stage in a show, or in front of a camera, I try to be honest in my intent, mine the material for clues about my character and make interesting choices for him, and find some new and unique way of delivering that information. It just makes it more fun and rewarding and a true "love" for acting can then be found and cultivated, which, I think is the real goal. Then, if some notoriety or accolades or "superstardom" comes from that, that's just an added bonus!

—WILL CHASE, (NBC'S *SMASH*; BROADWAY'S *RENT*, *AIDA*, AND *THE FULL MONTY*)

hile no one can deny the rush of adrenaline you get from being on stage, sometimes that feeling can be hard to come by—because you're waiting to be cast in a musical, or to be given a spot or a solo in a glee club.

Sometimes the best way to be creative is to start something yourself. Why wait for *them* to come to *you*? In this chapter you'll learn a few easy ways to help you take control over your own superstardom.

Let Me Entertain You

(*Gypsy*, 1959)

Let's say you have an awesome voice. Instead of waiting until auditions for the school musical come around, why not sit down at the piano and accompany yourself? Or, if you play guitar, strum along while you sing and be able to perform anytime, anywhere.

TIP: You don't need a stage to shine. Sometimes your very own basement, the patio in your backyard, or your parents' living room is the ideal place to start getting comfortable performing with a musical instrument.

Don't know how to play? Ask your parents for lessons as a birthday or holiday present. A few guitar lessons might not seem as exciting as some new clothes, but they'll get you a whole lot farther on the road to performing. If it's not possible for you to get lessons, there are books and instructional DVDs that teach you how to play some chords on the guitar, or scales on the piano. It may not seem like much at first, but every little bit counts.

Perhaps you already know how to play an instrument. Your local music store (or the Web) should have sheet music for your favorite artist's songs. Start by picking out songs you already know and love, and then practicing them at home. Like the

Beatles? Learn how to play "Across the Universe" for your friends. Want to practice your riffs? Snatch up some Mariah Carey songs and accompany yourself.

Even if you never wind up performing any of this music before an actual audience, practicing will only make you a more confident and skilled performer.

I Have Confidence

(*The Sound of Music*, 1965, Film)

Once you feel confident, you may be ready to start sharing your gift with others. It's great if your show choir has a concert or your school musical has a performance, but what if they don't—what then?

Enter: the Internet. Many performers get their start online. In 2010, Greyson Chance posted a video of himself performing an acoustic version of Lady Gaga's "Paparazzi." He became an overnight sensation, racking up millions of views on YouTube. Then Ellen DeGeneres called and invited him on her TV show. He wound up signing a record deal and releasing his music on iTunes.

Whether your purpose for posting videos is to earn a following or just good old fun, make sure you represent yourself in a way that you're proud of you. You just never know when a video is going to go viral!

"Going Viral": The passing and sharing of a video at a rapid fire pace. This type of video usually catapults a regular person into the public eye through an extreme amount of views in a short period of time and a great deal of Internet, possibly even television, buzz.

WARNING: Before you do anything that involves the Internet, it's incredibly important to make sure you have your parents' permission to do so. They'll help make sure that what you are doing is safe and legal.

HOW TO MAKE A YOUTUBE VIDEO

If you want to post a performance online, there's no better website to use than YouTube. So let's break down the process:

1. *Get permission from your parents!* You don't want your image or personal info to circulate worldwide if your parents don't approve. This isn't meant to scare you. Just be tasteful with how you represent yourself and don't share your life story in your *vlog* (as in video blog!).
2. *Edit your video.* Once you've shot your footage and decided on the material for the video, edit it the same way you'd proofread an essay for class. For example, you don't want there to be 45 seconds of "dead air" while you were washing your hands in the bathroom and didn't realize the camera was on. Also, with simple editing software like iMovie or Final Cut Pro you can add all kinds of effects. To spruce things up, consider adding credits, fancy transitions, or additional music or photos.
3. *Create a YouTube account.* When you're pleased with your edit, make yourself a YouTube account. (If you already have one, jump to #4.) Go to www.YouTube .com: At the top of the site there's an option to "Create an Account," so click on that! You'll need to provide a valid e-mail address, location, zip code, date of birth, gender, and then create a username and review the Terms of Service prior to accepting. Once you've followed these basic steps, click "I accept." The best part? Registering and maintaining an account is completely free!
4. *Upload!* Once your YouTube account is activated, it's time to make the video live. Log in—you'll see the option for "Upload" at the top of the screen. (If you edited with iMovie, make sure to export your video when you've finished the editing process.) YouTube gives the option of uploading a video or recording from a web-cam. When you click "Upload video," your computer will prompt you to locate the

video footage somewhere on your hard drive. Put your videos on your computer's desktop so they are easily accessible when it comes time for this crucial step.

5. ***Watch and enjoy.*** The video will take some time to finalize and the image will improve as it processes. When you're notified that the video is ready for viewing, check it out with your friends. This is your final chance to make sure you're pleased with the results.
6. ***Video's live and going viral.*** Once it's live, anyone and everyone can view, rate, and comment on your video.

Make sure that you're only uploading material that is original and that you've created. Any time you include someone else's work, you run the risk of infringing on their privacy. So for example, if you just rocked out with your buddy Steve on a tune he wrote, the considerate thing to do is ask his permission before uploading the new video. I'm 99.9% sure he'll say yes!

Once you know how to make a YouTube video, the possibilities are endless. Why not be like the kids on *iCarly* and have an Internet blog where you post videos of yourself performing?

There is one caveat, though: when you open yourself up to superstardom, there's also the possibility that you open yourself up to negative comments.

Some people will like what you do, and others won't. Don't worry about this; it's not your job to satisfy everyone's musical tastes. Simply do the very best that you can do, and be proud of your performance—whether it's singing, dancing, or playing in a band.

As long as you have a good support system of friends and family who believe in you and your talent, you should be fine. If you're afraid your feelings might get hurt, however, then posting videos online might not be right for you. Only *you* can know how you feel, so discuss these possibilities with an adult before moving forward.

Go Your Own Way

(Fleetwood Mac, 1976)

At some point, you might be interested in writing your own music. Great! There's nothing better than expressing your emotions in an artistic way.

Every traditional song has two things: music and lyrics.

LYRICS

The lyrics in a song are the words that tell the story. Even if you have a catchy melody, the words need to make sense and mean something to people. The best kinds of songs are ones where the lyrics are relatable, and talk about life experiences you've had that other people might have had, too.

For the most part, it makes sense to pick important subjects to write about. Some great topics for a song might be:

- Having a crush on someone, or falling in love
- How it feels when a person who is supposed to be your friend makes you feel bad or betrays your trust
- A time when you reached a goal or conquered a fear
- A time when you were happy (or sad) for a particular reason
- A wish or a dream you once had

Some topics that probably won't make a good song are:

- Your favorite stuffed animal
- A specific teacher you hate, and why
- A vacation you took with your family
- Your favorite food
- What TV shows you like to watch, or a movie you saw recently

The first list deals with meaningful emotions. It's broad enough that you can still make any of the choices very personal, but the actions listed—falling in love, getting your feelings hurt—are ones that play important roles in our everyday lives.

The second list, though, is too specific. Favorite stuffed animals? Teachers you hate? Maybe those could be lines within a song, but they probably won't make good subjects for an entire song because they aren't important enough.

TIP: You have to have a reason to write a song. If the subject isn't important to you, it won't be important to your audience.

Start by getting a journal and writing down your ideas. Buy something small that you can take with you anywhere—you never know when you might have a brilliant idea that you want to write down!

Sometimes people think lyrics to a song should be like poetry—this is certainly one way to go. But there's a fine line between saying how you feel and worrying too much about a pretty line. Remember: the most important thing is for your lyrics to be universal—meaningful to more than just you and your friends.

MUSIC

You don't need to be a concert pianist or know how to play a twelve-string guitar in order to write a great melody.

Sometimes you don't even need to know how to play an instrument at all—you can figure out how you'd like a song to go in your head. But it's definitely useful to have a basic understanding of music theory and chord progressions before you sit down and churn out hit song after hit song.

At first, stick to simple chords and easy melodies. There are many different ways to write a song, and this is an art—and a skill—that people practice for years. Everyone has to start somewhere.

And the place that you should start is with the classic AABA format.

This type of song has an opening section (A), a bridge (B), and then transitions to the final A section. A slew of musical genres use this format, including musical theater, pop, and jazz.

An AABA song will look like this, more or less:

A = 8 bars

A = 8 bars

B = 8 bars

A = 8 bars

The first two A sections will have the same melody, only with different lyrics. Letter B will be your bridge, which is where the melody changes—this section also has different lyrics than anything that came before it. And then you end with the (now) familiar A section.

Let's see how this works in an actual song. Take the Irving Berlin classic "What'll I Do." If you don't know the song, give it a quick listen before continuing:

A = What'll I do when you are far away . . .

A = What'll I do when I am wond'ring who . . .

B = What'll I do with just a photograph . . .

A = When I'm alone with only dreams . . .

When you listen, you'll recognize that the A sections have the same melody, but different lyrics. The B section—the bridge—has different lyrics and a different melody.

Remember that this is only one type of song, and there are many wonderful exceptions to this rule. But it should give you a jumping-off point to start writing!

SEVEN EASY STEPS TO SONGWRITING

Blair Bodine, a professional singer and songwriter based in Nashville, is a beautiful storyteller who writes gorgeous country tunes. She's provided her "Seven Easy Steps to Songwriting" that will help out any newbie who has a penchant for making music.

1. **BE PREPARED.** This motto isn't just for Boy Scouts! All the best artists and writers I know always have a pencil and paper ready to go. Write down every song idea or neat phrase that pops into your mind. Many cell phones and computers have built-in recorders. Use these to capture melodies that come to you. You never know when your next song will show up!

2. **STAY INSPIRED.** Sometimes, inspiration hits you like a lightning bolt. The rest of the time, it is up to you as an artist to stay inspired. Surround yourself with music, art, or poetry. It's also great to have your own space to create, whether it's a corner of your room that you decorate, or a picnic table at a local park surrounded by nature. Find that space, and know you can always return there to center yourself and create.

3. **REVISIT YOUR VISIONS.** When you encounter writer's block, as you most certainly will, you may feel like your creative well is dry. It's not! Revisit all your song snippets, ideas, and melodies from Step 1. You're more prolific than you thought you were!

→

4. **PLAY WELL WITH OTHERS.** Whether it's cowriting a song, forming a band, or just sharing ideas, my greatest ideas (and greatest friendships) have sprung from collaboration. Is there a great poet in your class? An amazing painter? Get together and see what creative ideas you can cook up.

5. **PERFECT YOUR CRAFT.** There's an old joke that goes, "*Do you know how to get to Carnegie Hall*?" It's easy. Just practice, practice, practice. The truth is, if you want to be a superstar that shines, you've got to put in the time. In addition to practicing and writing each day, create miniexercises for yourself. Write a song in ten minutes. Write a song where every line begins with the letter Q. Find fun ways to challenge yourself, and you'll be amazed at what you can do!

6. **DEVELOP YOUR STYLE.** Johnny Cash once told his daughter, Rosanne, "Style is a function of your limitations, more so than a function of your skills." Can't hit the high notes? Worried that your piano skills don't match your vocal chops? It doesn't matter! The most interesting vocalists and musicians know their limitations and use them to their advantage. Leonard Cohen would have gotten an F in chorus class. Paul McCartney, one of the most revered songwriters of all time, can't read music! Who cares? You may wake up one day and realize, what holds you back is actually what propels you forward.

7. **SHARE YOUR SONG.** Personally, I would have never been able to travel the world and play music for thousands of people, if I had never emerged from my bedroom (my favorite place to write and sing) and gone to my first open mike. It may sound scary

to get out there and share your songs, but it's worth it! One of the best parts about open mike culture is the supportive environment. Tell people it is your first time playing, and they will cheer you wildly! Trust me. Every superstar songwriter has a story about the first time they played their own song in public. What will yours be?

For more information about Blair, visit www.blairbodine.com.

Strike Up the Band

(*Strike Up the Band*, 1930)

Maybe you'd like a taste of the spotlight, but you're not interested in being a superstar on your own. A band could be the perfect thing for you.

Much like a show choir or glee club, a band combines a love for music with a sense of community—your band mates are your friends and can even be a pseudo-family. If you're lucky, your school will already have an extracurricular organization like a band, orchestra, or choir that you can join.

If your school *doesn't*—or even if it does, and you want something extra!—don't worry. Start one on your own. This may seem daunting, but really it's simple.

1. Figure out what you want your group to be like. Are you a singer looking to put together a band? A guitar player looking for someone to jam with? A dancer looking to choreograph a routine? Whatever it is, be clear about your goals.

   TIP: Go to a teacher in your school (preferably someone in the arts department). Chances are, other kids have spoken about the very same thing and your teacher can put you in touch with them directly.

2. Once you've talked to a faculty member, get your masking tape ready! Make a

poster to hang up on some of the bulletin boards: SUPERSTARS WANTED!

3. Ask one of the music teachers if you can make an announcement during a scheduled class or rehearsal. You can even go to your student government representatives and see if it's possible to advertise on the morning announcements.
4. An easy way to spread the word about your musical/artistic desires is simply to vocalize them. Tell your friends that you want to start a band—soon it will become a topic of conversation. Maybe someone will overhear you in the cafeteria, or randomly mention the same thing to one of your friends. You never know!

The more you talk about your goals—to start a band, to choreograph a dance—the more likely they are to become a reality.

Express Yourself

(Flora the Red Menace, 1965)

Whether you're a solo performer or you've just gotten your band together and you've been rehearsing, the most important thing? Get out there and strut your stuff!

One day you'll be playing at Madison Square Garden performing for thousands of people. Until then, any performance opportunity is one that you should take.

Coffee Shops: Is there a local independent shop near your house? Chances are they have open mike nights—check one out and see if you can audition and play a song or two. It's a great way to practice performing in front of a live audience, work the kinks out of your music, and see what people respond to.

Home: No open mike night? Perform anywhere—even in your living room! Ask your parents if you can entertain their guests during a party or when their friends are over for dinner. Is one of your friends having a birthday? Why not be the entertainment?

School: Undoubtedly, a talent show is a fantastic place to shine. Don't be afraid to show your classmates your star quality! You can even sing a cappella. The important thing is that you get practice—because the more you perform, the better a performer you will become. It's as simple as that.

If your school doesn't have a talent show, why not organize one? Check in with the music department, student government, or any faculty member about doing so. Part of being a superstar is about creating opportunities to showcase your talent and demonstrate how much you truly shine.

But be ready: once you give people a taste of the superstar inside you, they'll be following you around nonstop, beginning for more!

CHAPTER TWELVE
Backstage Pass
ADMIT ONE
66928

We are *all* superstars. From the way we treat people in the supermarket, how we conduct ourselves riding the subway and our everyday living—our lives reflect our stardom. Those who stand out—the super-"superstars"—are those who possess a talent most peculiar and enriching. This talent brings down a house with her belting beautiful voice; it gives the chills to grown adults when he hoofs and taps his heart away on a bare stage to nothing but the beat of his own song; this talent stops the show, and holds an audience in emotional suspense until it is too much . . . and finally lets that audience take a breath. It is exuberating to all involved. To me, however, what really makes a "SuperStar" is a performer's willingness to share honestly and truthfully with the people directly in front of them. A "SuperStar" knows their own worth and doesn't flaunt it in the face of others. A "SuperStar" must first become acquainted with their beautiful and unique gifts, then selflessly share those gifts with the rest of us. That is when the "SuperStar" is catapulted into SuperStardom.

—CHAD KIMBALL,
TONY AND DRAMA DESK NOMINEE FOR *MEMPHIS*

Congratulations! By now you've figured out a slew of different techniques to help you prepare for superstardom. But what if you don't want to be a performer? Perhaps you dream of being *behind* the spotlight. If that's the case, this is the perfect chapter for you.

Every musical has a director, musical director, and choreographer who help bring the show to life. They teach the actors and musicians the songs, figure out where the actors should stand and what their motivations should be, as well as what the entire production should look like—along with the help of lighting and sound designers, stage managers, and many, many more.

This doesn't just go for musicals, either. Every music video you see has a director and a choreographer. If you go to see a performer like Christina Aguilera or Bruno Mars in concert, that show has a lighting designer, a stage manager, and well—the list is practically never ending.

Each of these roles, while very different, is equally important.

DIRECTOR

The director is the leader in all respects of the production. The director is responsible for assembling a strong team of artistic people to make the performance and technical elements of the production gel. Standard responsibilities for a school's director include:

1. Picking the musical/dramatic production.
2. Holding auditions and casting the show.
3. Organizing a rehearsal schedule.
4. Giving the actors blocking and assisting them with character development.
5. Collaborating with the musical director and choreographer to establish a cohesive through line.

6. Defining an artistic vision to communicate to the costume, sound, set, and lighting designers.

The director usually seeks help in the form of an assistant. An assistant director is the director's right-hand man. The "AD" helps with artistic decisions and takes

DIRECTING TRIO

Steven Spielberg

Arguably one of the most legendary film directors/producers of all time, Spielberg is the artistic visionary behind film classics like *Jurassic Park*, *E.T.*, *Indiana Jones*, *Jaws*, *Schindler's List*, and the TV show *Smash*.

Julie Taymor

You may know Julie Taymor's body of work from the Broadway smash hit *The Lion King*, which brought innovative puppetry to the musical stage. She also was the original director for *Spider-Man: Turn off the Dark* and the film *Across the Universe*, and was a production consultant for Michael Jackson's *This Is It* concert tour in 2009.

Trevor Nunn

A major force in the industry, this British director has had several stage productions on Broadway and the West End, earning multiple Tony and Olivier Awards. His major shows include *Les Misérables*, *Starlight Express*, *Copenhagen*, and *Sunset Boulevard*. In addition to directing *Cats*, he also provided additional lyrics to the song "Memory."

notes to help the director. Many schools may have student-run programs where upper and lower classmen mimic the relationship between a director and the AD.

If not, approach the head director about assisting a production. And if your school doesn't already have a student-run program, why not start one yourself?

DIRECTOR CHECKLIST

Artistic Vision: The director must carefully examine and consider the "Who," "What," "When," "Where," and "Why" in all respects. The acting style, costumes, and other technical elements must fit consistently within the show's setting.

Leadership Skills: Taking charge, being diplomatic and smart with regards to the production values. A great leader is also sensitive to the needs of his fellow artists, actors, musicians, and stagehands.

Team Player Attitude: The director must know how to collaborate and incorporate the talents of others to create a cohesive project.

Organization: Organization is key for a director to run a tight ship!

CHOREOGRAPHER

The choreographer is essential in a musical production or dance routine.

In a heavy dance show, the choreographer's responsibility is to create elaborate dance routines that fit the music and emotional mood of the show. In a show where fewer dance numbers are required, a choreographer will move the various actors around the stage during musical numbers.

Oftentimes the director and choreographer are the same person because the two jobs are simultaneously needed to create seamless transitions and visualize a complete stage picture. Taking on both major roles at once ultimately makes everyone's life easier. Some examples of top-notch Broadway director/choreographers include:

Rob Ashford (*Promises, Promises; How to Succeed in Business Without Really Trying*)

Michael Bennett (*Seesaw, A Chorus Line, Ballroom, Dreamgirls*)

Bob Fosse (*Redhead, Little Me, Sweet Charity, Pippin, Chicago, Dancin', Big Deal*)

Kathleen Marshall (*Wonderful Town, The Pajama Game, Grease, Anything Goes*)

Casey Nicholaw (*The Drowsy Chaperone, Elf, The Book of Mormon*)

Susan Stroman (*Contact, The Producers, Young Frankenstein, The Scottsboro Boys*)

Inspired by any of the above? Consider sharing your gifts through a talent show, competitive dance team, dance club, or dance show. These experiences differ from a musical since they're not telling one main story. Choreographers often need assistants to help run auditions and teach the dance routines throughout the rehearsal process. If you don't want complete dance authority but think you may want to shadow, seek out an assistant choreography position.

CHOREOGRAPHER CHECKLIST

Dance Knowledge: Being a trained dancer will certainly help. You don't have to be the best technician to express your art but knowing the vocabulary will give you common ground with your dancers.

Special Awareness: Maybe you like to paint or take photos? Have a great eye for landscapes and backdrops? Choreographers need to organize bodies on a stage and your keen eye will lend itself well to creating visually stimulating pictures.

Sensitivity and Patience: A choreographer deals with body image, and in a school environment all shapes and sizes are welcome. Choreographers want anyone with a heart for dance.

Artistic Vision: Choreographers must tell a story with their routines. It is typical for dance pieces to incorporate music to support the storytelling. With the help of good lighting, dancers must express how they feel with their bodies and faces.

MUSICAL DIRECTOR

The musical director is responsible for teaching the music and honoring the score in its original form. The "MD" is generally the one that gives vocal coaching to the actors as they learn their material, rehearses with the musicians in the pit, and conducts the orchestra. Typically, the musical director must play the piano.

Show choir, vocal jazz ensemble, glee club, a cappella, and most types of singing groups also have musical directors. Someone needs to be in charge of picking out the songs and creating the musical arrangements. You may be the perfect candidate for musical direction if you love to play instruments but have no interest in singing. General knowledge of music theory, music history, and voice types will serve you tremendously in this role.

MUSICAL DIRECTOR CHECKLIST

Reads Music: A musical director dissects the score of a show and can communicate to each instrumentalist whether the music is in bass or treble clef. A comprehensive understanding of keys, scales, and voice parts is required.

Musicality: An MD must have a great ear and sense of rhythm. He/she should be able to recognize a group dynamic and highlight its greatest qualities.

Open Mind: Let's face it—not every musician or vocalist will have the ability to hit all the notes, licks, and riffs as originally written into the score. It's up to the performer and MD to find a happy medium that suits the performer's skill set. If there's a difficult saxophone run or some notes are way too low for a singer, the MD will come up with an alternative so everyone looks good. And when a performer is really lucky, the MD will change a key altogether to enhance his or her performance.

Rob Berman

Rob Berman is currently the musical director of the *Encores!* series at City Center in New York City. Recent Broadway credits include conductor of *A Man of No Importance* (Lincoln Center), and musical director of *The Pajama Game* and *Wonderful Town*.

Here's how he defines the challenging role of a musical director:

A musical director on Broadway has a more complex job than most people probably realize. The musical director is the head of the music department on a show, and depending on whether it is a revival or a new show, the duties range from collaborating on what the songs should be, to how the songs should sound, how they should be sung, how the dance music is constructed, where is there underscoring or reprises, how big is the orchestra, who should play in the orchestra, what kind of singers should be in the ensemble. . . . It goes on and on. A musical director must have great taste and understanding of the style of the piece he or she is working on.

COSTUME DESIGNER

Are you the hipster funky type who's always cutting up your T-shirts, sewing on patches, bedazzling sweatshirts, ripping up your jeans, or cutting your hair in trendy styles? If you look forward to swapping clothes with your friends or running around the mall acting like a personal stylist to your family, then your fashion forward inventiveness could mean you're destined to be a costume designer.

The costume designer is one of the main leaders in the visual aesthetic of the production. Some questions a costume designer may ask when examining a character are:

1. Does he take care of his physical appearance?
2. Is she very poor? Ultra rich?
3. Is the climate hot? Cold? Moderate?

These details make the story specific and give the audience a clear understanding of the plot. The designer must research the time period to understand the political and social climate of each setting.

The technique and artistry of the job include expertise in sewing and stitching, body awareness, color coordination, and fabric knowledge. But if you're inexperienced in any of these areas, don't shy away. A great designer is eager to mentor and will gladly teach you the tricks of the trade!

In the case of the school show, the costume designer may be a teacher or someone's parent. The designer could always use an assistant or a wardrobe crew that is responsible for maintaining the well-being of the costumes. The role of the dresser/wardrobe crew is great for someone interested in costumes but not particularly keen on being responsible for the entire production. They are strategically placed backstage, assigned to performers and ready to assist in a fast-paced theatrical zone.

STAGE MANAGER

A stage manager (SM) is responsible for running all technical elements of a show, and is the major organizer of all scheduling functions. There are five key phases of a show that help define a stage manager's job: pre-production, rehearsals, tech, running a show, and post-production.

Christy Ney

Christy Ney has worked as a stage manager on Broadway shows like *Wicked* and *The Lion King*. She says:

A Stage Manager's responsibilities morph and change through each stage of the show and even on a daily basis.

During pre-production, when analyzing the script, the SM looks for information that will help create and support the show such as: the props that are used and how they function, the time of day and locations that the show requires, the technical needs, costume needs, and any sound, music, or special effects that the script calls for.

Before rehearsals begin, the SMs set up the look and feel of the rehearsal space(s). They organize the rehearsal props, furniture, and costume pieces and set up the tables and chairs for the director and Stage Management team to work from. They also put together scripts, score copies, and welcome packets for the company members.

During the rehearsal process, the SMs are responsible for tracking all props, costumes, set moves, desired lighting, sound, and special effect cues. The SMs are also responsible for taking "blocking"—a written record of all of the actors' movements throughout the show—script changes, and scheduling.

The tech period is when the technical and physical elements of the show come together with the actors in the theater for the very first time. Questions that arise during tech are: Where do the actors change costumes? Where does an actor need to stand in order to be safe yet lit properly? How do we get someone around a set piece and up a staircase to make an entrance? Ultimately, tech is about creating a safe and secure environment for the actors and staff as they work to bring the show to life.

When the show is running, a SM is responsible for maintaining the creative team's artistic vision night after night. One of the ways that this is accomplished is through calling the sequence of cues for each show. He/she wears a headset and is able to verbally and visually (through the use of cue lights) communicate with the other Stage Managers (if your production requires more than one), the Head Carpenter(s), Sound Engineer, Conductor, Light Board Operator, and Spotlight Operators.

Post-production is the period of time after the show closes. The SM assists in organizing and clearing out offices and dressing rooms, completing and "cleaning up" paperwork, and possibly even striking the set. Once this work is accomplished, the SM is now ready to move on to the next show!

PROPS AND SET DESIGN/CONSTRUCTION

Back in your early days were you a big fan of blocks, LEGOs, or K'NEX? How about playing with tiny model airplanes, train sets, or making dioramas for class projects? If so, this hands-on job might be right up your alley! Props and set design/construction give you an "in" with the theatrical family while also creating pieces of art.

The set designer is responsible for researching the time period of the show and creating a look for the stage that establishes a specific setting. He or she may ask:

1. What city, country, and time period is it?
2. How many scenes are inside versus outside?
3. Is the setting going to be a literal or abstract representation of the period?

The set designer and director work hand in hand to honor the script but also may take artistic liberties. For example, not every version of *Romeo & Juliet* you will see takes places in the Elizabethan era. Sometimes a director's concept is to modernize a well-known classic such that *R + J* could take place in California with guns and cars (Hello, Baz Luhrmann!), rather than swords and horses.

Set designers have been educated in fine arts, architecture, drawing, and sketching. They create a floor plan that the construction crew builds. Knowledge of theatrical spaces is essential so designers can be conscious of the actors' safety when sketching platforms and other structures. Working with a hammer, drill, saw, and all kinds of tools come into play with this job.

The construction crew may also double as the running crew that moves furniture around during scene changes. This is a good job for someone who likes to be around the cast and is able to attend every performance. You will be needed during blackouts in between scenes to make swift transitions.

The prop master is a fantastic job for someone who is very crafty or resourceful. A prop can be just about anything that an actor uses in a scene that isn't part of the set. For example, when performing "Adelaide's Lament" in *Guys and Dolls*, Adelaide keeps sneezing and needs a tissue handy. This tissue is therefore a prop; she needs it to simulate a real-life action, which in turn makes the audience laugh.

Dannielle Robertson

Dannielle Robertson, performer from the original films of *My Fair Lady* and *Oliver!*, has lent her fine arts skills to such movie sets as *Edward Scissorhands* and *Jurassic Park*. Here is her five-step building process:

I initially meet with the director to get her "vision" for the production where I:

1. Block out the sets and scenes with the director.

2. Embrace the director's vision with what is feasible to create given the talent and budget.

3. Create a materials list for the director to approve and a build schedule.

4. Build and paint the sets for a show. Some directors like to use pre-painted backdrops, so I may have to design in proportion for those drops.

5. Create environments for each scene and speak with the lighting director, allowing him to give it over to his students to create the mood required with effects or gels.

Once a show has ended, the designers and construction team hang back to deconstruct the set in a process called *strike*. What took weeks to build is gone in hours. Oh well—nothing lasts forever!

SOUND DESIGNER

A sound designer is responsible for managing the audio balance in a production. He adjusts the levels of microphones used by singers and musicians so the blend is appropriate and pleasing to the ear.

In theater, aside from making sure every bit of dialogue and song is beautifully captured, sound designers are also responsible for adding other sound effects to the environment. Whenever a noise is needed like a honking horn, baby crying, or fire truck siren, the sound designer finds the most accurate replica so that it is believable.

EXAMPLE: If two actors are fighting on stage and are directed to break something fragile, glass won't *actually* shatter on stage for safety purposes. Instead, the actors are trained to give the illusion of broken glass through body actions and the technicians take care of the sound effects and special props.

FACT: In a rock show or talent show, the microphone placement on the stage and the overall amplification of the music is an art in and of itself because it affects your emotional experience as an audience member.

LIGHTING DESIGNER

A lighting designer ensures that everything is visible, creating a general mood that reflects the tone of the writing, music, and acting, as well as the time period in which the show is set. A lighting designer is responsible for knowing the color palate and how to operate a lighting board. Lighting can range from subtle, so as not to pull focus from the scene, to very drastic when going for a laugh or dramatic shift.

Zach Blane

Zach Blane, a professional lighting designer, offers great insight on all aspects of lighting design:

I suggest reading plays and exposing yourself to different forms of art. Paintings, sculptures, music, anything to get the creative juices flowing! I highly recommend ***Stage Lighting Design: The Art, the Craft, the Life*** by Richard Pilbrow for young artists who are looking to get their feet wet.

A common misconception pertaining to lighting is that it is all tech and no design. Of course there are many technical aspects to it, but lighting is as much of an artistic expression as any other medium. The lighting generally comes from the text. If I were to set up the lighting for the famous balcony scene in ***Romeo & Juliet***, what do I think about? Moonlight, textural large walls, exterior garden light, candlelight from within Juliet's bedroom, face light for Juliet on the balcony, and face light for Romeo on the ground. What does the sky look like—are stars glistening, or is it cloudy?

All of these notions are what make up the whole stage picture. First you must think of your final product and then figure out what equipment is needed to accomplish that look, using the light plot. Design is an art and I consider myself a painter. The lights are my paintbrushes.

Once the stage picture is set, a lighting designer must finesse the "internal" cues. For example, how do I subconsciously pull to the balcony after Romeo has climbed it, without the audience physically noticing a change?

Lighting design expresses the psychology of the piece. It is the foundation in which the show is presented to an audience. It can hide things you don't want them to see and highlight things you do. Designers are like magicians, taking the spectator on a journey by guiding them with a sleight of hand.

TIP: Another job for someone interested in lighting might be the spotlight operator. This is the person that literally focuses the spotlight on individual performers during their shining moments.

Intrigued by any of these positions? Check out the documentary *Show Business: The Road to Broadway*. It's a behind-the-scenes look at the creative process for *Wicked; Taboo*; *Caroline, Or Change*; and *Avenue Q*. And it's available on DVD.

As you can tell, a show's success depends on many technical elements. So it's time to flash your backstage pass and discover a new artistic voyage!

Finale

Now that you know more about various performing arts opportunities and have gained helpful auditioning tips and advice, what's the best thing you can do?

Believe in yourself and let your inner star shine brightly.

Whether you want to hear your original songs on the radio or dance on Broadway or simply have a little bit of extracurricular fun, confidence is key: you are talented and important, and you deserve a shot at whatever artistic opportunity you want to be a part of just as much as anyone else.

Sure, putting yourself out there can be scary. If you don't, though, you'll never be able to share your talents with your friends, family, and community. If performing and the arts is something important to you, then you must let people know.

There is a superstar in everyone.

Now go find yours!

Encore

Now that you've finished reading this book and honed your skills at home, take the next step and explore some summer camp, pre-college, and scholarship opportunities! The following lists are by no means complete, so it's still worth taking the time to research on your own.

Happy hunting, superstars!

Summer Camps and Theater Intensives

There are incredible summer camps and theater intensive programs all over the country that incorporate pre-professional training, allowing students to immerse themselves in an artistic community and focus on what they love to do.

BLUE LAKE FINE ARTS CAMP (MICHIGAN)
www.bluelake.org

BRITISH AMERICAN DRAMA ACADEMY (ENGLAND)
www.badaonline.com

BROADWAY DREAMS FOUNDATION (USA)
www.mybroadwaydreams.com

BROADWAY THEATRE PROJECT (FLORIDA)
www.broadwaytheatreproject.com

FRENCH WOODS FESTIVAL (NEW YORK)
www.frenchwoods.com

GRAMMY CAMP (USA)
www.grammyintheschools.com

IDYLLWILD ARTS (CALIFORNIA)
www.idyllwildarts.org

INTERLOCHEN CENTER FOR THE ARTS (MICHIGAN)
www.interlochen.org

PERRY MANSFIELD PERFORMING ARTS CAMP (COLORADO)
www.perry-mansfield.org

YOUNG PEOPLE'S SUMMER STOCK (MARYLAND)
www.gfs.org

STAGE DOOR MANOR (NEW YORK)
www.stagedoormanor.com

WALNUT HILL (MASSACHUSETTS)
www.walnuthillarts.org

Pre-College Programs

Just like the above-mentioned summer camps, many colleges offer programs that simulate their BA/BFA training schedules taught by the professors who teach undergraduate courses.

These programs might be ideal for high school students.

UNIVERSITY OF THE ARTS (PENNSYLVANIA)
www.uarts.edu

CALIFORNIA STATE SUMMER SCHOOL FOR THE ARTS
calarts.edu/campus/CSSSA
www.innerspark.us

CARNEGIE MELLON PRE-COLLEGE (PENNSYLVANIA)
www.cmu.edu/enrollment/pre-college

UNIVERSITY OF MICHIGAN: MPULSE
www.music.umich.edu/special_programs/youth

NORTHWESTERN UNIVERSITY: CHERUBS (ILLINOIS)
www.northwestern.edu/nhsi

OKLAHOMA CITY UNIVERSITY (OKLAHOMA)
www.okcu.edu/music/academy

THE JUILLIARD SCHOOL PRE-COLLEGE DIVISION (NEW YORK)
www.juilliard.edu/youth-adult/pre-college

Scholarships and National Recognition

If you're starting to think about college, take a look at some of these scholarship opportunities.

NATIONAL FOUNDATION FOR ADVANCEMENT IN THE ARTS (NFAA) | WWW.YOUNGARTS.ORG

The National Foundation for Advancement in the Arts created **YOUNGARTS**, the "signature national organization that recognizes and supports America's most talented 17–18 year olds in visual, literary, and performing arts." Every year 150 students, spanning nine disciplines, are invited by competitive screening to a weeklong celebration in Miami to take workshops with various industry professionals from Hollywood, Broadway, and the music and fine arts industries.

YOUNGARTS is also the exclusive organization in nominating the nation's Presidential Scholar in the Arts, the highest honor for any young artist to receive. Presidential Scholars are invited to a White House ceremony and perform at the John F. Kennedy Center for the Performing Arts.

THE NATIONAL HIGH SCHOOL MUSICAL THEATER AWARDS (NHSMTA) | WWW.NHSMTA.COM

"The **NATIONAL HIGH SCHOOL MUSICAL THEATER AWARDS** is a national celebration of outstanding student achievement recognizing individual artistry in vocal, dance, and acting performance. The program aims to create a pathway connecting promising young performers to the professional theater industry. The program is the year-end culmination of awards programs across the country presented by dozens of professional theater organizations. Finalists in New York are named Best Actress or Best Actor at a regional competition, representing approximately 1,000 schools. While in New York City, participants experience five days of private coaching, master classes, and rehearsals with theater professionals. Students receive opportunities for merit scholarships, professional advancement, and other prizes."

INTERNATIONAL THESPIAN SOCIETY | SCHOOLTHEATRE.ORG/EVENTS/FESTIVAL

Each troupe is led by a troupe director who is a professional member of the Educational Theater Association. The troupe director is typically—but not always—the theater teacher in the school. Students earn an invitation to Thespian Society membership on the basis of their achievements in the school's theater program.

ENGLISH-SPEAKING UNION NATIONAL SHAKESPEARE COMPETITION | WWW.ESUUS.ORG/PROGRAMS_SHAKESPEARE_COMPETITION.HTM

"The program begins in classrooms nationwide. A school-wide competition is held in the Fall/Winter, where students perform a monologue from one of Shakespeare's plays. The school competition winner then advances to the ESU Branch (community) Competition in the Winter. There the student performs his/her monologue and one of Shakespeare's sonnets. The Branch Competition winner then advances to the National Competition held in New York City in the Spring. The student performs his/her monologue and sonnet at Lincoln Center in front of their fellow contestants from across the country. Seven to ten students are then chosen for the final round of the Competition; they perform their selections along with a cold reading of a monologue later in the day for another round of judges. Each Branch winner receives an all-expenses-paid trip to New York City, to compete at the National Competition at Lincoln Center. The trip also includes exclusive workshops, sightseeing, and interacting with other Branch winners from across the country. The winner of the ESU National Shakespeare Competition receives an all-expenses-paid trip to study acting in Shakespeare's homeland, England."

SPOTLIGHT AWARDS | MUSICCENTER.ORG/EDUCATION/SPOT_INDEX.HTML

The Music Center's Spotlight program is for high school students in the visual and performing arts in Southern California. With an emphasis on self-esteem, preparation, and perseverance, this unique learning experience provides a community of support for the development of young artists to help strengthen artistic and performance skills.

The Spotlight performance categories are ballet, non-classical dance, classical voice, non-classical voice, classical instrumental music, and jazz instrumental music. The visual arts are included with the two-dimensional art and photography categories.

Summer Stock Programs

Theaters all over the country encourage young people to audition for their summer seasons. Companies typically invite students eighteen years and older to participate in their seasons and take on chorus positions or featured roles. Many companies provide housing, salaries, and points for Equity Membership Candidacy program. Oftentimes a core group of young performers is hired to participate in many of the shows in a rotating repertory schedule or "summer stock" experience. This method develops a family atmosphere and a sense of community within the company.

Attending a theater conference is a great way to audition for multiple companies at once, which greatly increases the chances of booking a job. All of the conferences listed below are combined audition opportunities where you can meet various industry professionals in one location.

NEW ENGLAND THEATRE CONFERENCE (MASSACHUSETTS)
www.netconline.org

STRAWHAT AUDITIONS (NEW YORK)
www.strawhat-auditions.com

SOUTHEASTERN THEATRE CONFERENCE (GEORGIA)
www.setc.org

UNITED PROFESSIONAL THEATRE AUDITIONS (TENNESSEE)
www.upta.org

Author's Note

The inspiration for this book came from my years as a performer. Without the encouragement and training I received, I would never have grown into the person I am today.

Special thanks to Nina Pfeffer, who gave me the opportunity to shine and pushed me to become better every day that I attended Herricks High School. I wish that all young "superstars" could have someone like Nina to believe in them. Countless hours were spent rehearsing for musical or show choir concerts, singing during lunch period, and traveling to and from performances. I will always be indebted to you for your kindness, skill, and unwavering ability to bring the best out of me.

Junior year of high school, I auditioned for the Juilliard School Pre-College Division. Lorraine Nubar saw something special in me and accepted me into the program, and Andrew Thomas made it feasible for me to attend. At Juilliard, Lorraine taught me how to sing—and appreciate—classical music. I am forever grateful for her training, and for her warm and loving personality. Jorge Parodi helped me to fine-tune my skills and interpret many a song. And to the many wonderful teachers I had during my two years at Pre-College: thank you.

As a high school senior, I was selected by the National Foundation for Advancement in the Arts to travel to Miami as part of their YoungArts program. There, I met other singers and artists who shared similar beliefs and passions. It was one of the most extraordinary weeks of my life, and cemented my love for music. I still keep in touch with many of the friends I made there, and am delighted to be able to donate proceeds of this book to the foundation so that other aspiring artists will be able to reach for the stars. A few months after I attended, I received the biggest honor of my life: I was selected as a Presidential Scholar in the Arts. I spent a week in Washington, DC, performed at the Kennedy Center, and was awarded a medal from the vice president. Thank you to NFAA for making so many of my dreams come true.

When I was accepted to Juilliard as an undergraduate, I studied with Marlena Malas. It wasn't easy at first; at times it felt like I had no idea what I was doing. But eventually I realized that what I was doing was growing. Changing. Evolving as a singer and musician. I have never forgotten the invaluable lessons I learned while under her tutelage, and I consider myself incredibly lucky to have been her student.

I have recently met new teachers who have helped me to rediscover my inner superstar. Brad Ross, Devin Ilaw, Jen Waldman, and Sharon Kenny have been invaluable, and Josh Pultz has shown me that dreams really do come true.

Lastly, being a performer is nearly impossible without a support team: thanks to my mother and father, Elizabeth and Steven Malawer; my grandmother, Eileen Honigman; my sister, Abby Malawer; my uncles Alan and Mark; and the rest of my Honigman family, especially Aunt Laurie and Leigh, all of whom attended many performances over the years and always loved to hear me sing.

Ted Michael

Acknowledgments

Special thanks to the artists featured in this book for giving our "superstars" great slice-of-life anecdotes and words of wisdom from your extensive careers.

Many helping hands offered their advice, expertise, and contact lists. They include: Tiffany Bartok, Josh Breckenridge, Jennifer Lauren Brown, Joyce Chittick, Lauryn Ciardullo, Susan Corrado, Ken Davenport, Lynda DeFuria, Ron DeMaio, Jeremiah Downes, Sean Patrick Doyle, Stephanie Gibson, Giulia Griffith, Matthew Growdon, Megan Harmon and the 2011 YoungArts Theater finalists, Andrew Hodge, Star Kahn, Nathan Klau, Michael Linden, Kristoffer Lowe, Jesse Manocherian, Cameron Neilson, Celia Mei Rubin, Michael Silberblatt, Dani Spieler, George Stiles, Wesley Taylor, and Jake Wilson.

FROM NIC: I would like to thank Grandma Grace for the smiles, Grandma Faye for the pearls of wisdom, Sister for being my #1 fan, and Joe S. for the phone calls. Thanks to "the ladies"—especially J-M, Devin, Matthew and Finks—for the constant support. I'm grateful to Benjamin and Brandon for being my West Coast brothers. Thanks to Mara for her undying enthusiasm and encyclopedic knowledge. I am forever grateful to the professors who have helped pave my creative path, especially Claudia Benack, Thomas Douglas, and Barbara MacKenzie-Wood. To Mom and Dad: thank you for always believing in me and for trusting the "leap of faith" I made you take with me seven years ago. And, of course, thanks to Ted, for making it all happen.

FROM MARA: I'd like to thank my mom, Emmi, for giving me the creative writing gene. She is my inspiration and trusty editor. Thanks to Erika, Scott, Dad, and my extended family for their constant support and for seeing every one of my shows. Thanks to an endless list of friends who sent e-mails and contacted our fellow "show people." Thanks to the *Veendam* cast and crew: You were by my side during the bulk of this creative process from L.A. at the Madrid to Docksider in Bermuda. Many extraordinary teachers encouraged me to perform and write through the years. STAC, French Woods Festival, UArts, and other wonderful theatrical experiences have shaped the artist that I am today. Nic, thank you for sharing your knowledge and collaborating on this project. And finally, Ted. From Sad Girl to your Albert in *Bye Bye Birdie* at Herricks Middle School through Liesl to your Rolf in *The Sound of Music* at Forestburgh Playhouse, we have shared so many great memories on stage and off. Now transitioning from stage to page, thank you for fostering my passion, craft, and talent by taking a chance on me with this book!

FROM TED: I would like to thank the incomparable Lea Salonga for sharing her stories and giving *Superstar* her stamp of approval. Thanks to Beverly Horowitz and Jennifer Joel for their helpful comments; Josh Pultz for his encouragement and unwavering support; and to Nic and Mara, two of the most talented writers and performers I have had the pleasure of working with.

Finally, an epic round of applause to Lisa Cheng for believing in this project and shepherding it to publication with great care, intelligence, and enthusiasm. Susan Hom ensured it was clean and precise, while Frances Soo Ping Chow's artistic vision made it sing. The phenomenal team at Running Press Kids made it possible for this book to get into your hands, and for that we are forever grateful.

About the Author

TED MICHAEL was born in 1984 and grew up in Roslyn Heights, New York. A 2002 Presidential Scholar in the Arts, he is also a graduate of Columbia University and The Juilliard School, and has performed Off-Broadway and with major opera companies and regional theaters across the country. Ted has published two novels, *The Diamonds* and *Crash Test Love*, a Seventeen.com Beach Read and a Books-A-Million Book Club Pick.

Most importantly, perhaps, Ted has performed in numerous show choirs and a cappella groups, as well as several high school musicals.

You can visit him online at www.tedmichaelbooks.com.

About the Contributors

LEA SALONGA is a singer and actress who is best known for her Tony Award–winning role in *Miss Saigon*. She is recognized for having won, in addition to the Tony, the Olivier, Drama Desk, Outer Critics Circle, and Theatre World Awards. In 2002, she took on the role of a Chinese immigrant in a reinterpretation of Rodgers and Hammerstein's *Flower Drum Song*, on Broadway. She was also the first Asian to play Éponine in the musical *Les Misérables* on Broadway and returned to the beloved show as Fantine in the 2006 revival. She began her career as a child star in the Philippines, making her professional debut in 1978 at the age of seven in the musical *The King and I*. She went on to star in productions of *Annie*, *Cat on a Hot Tin Roof*, *Fiddler on the Roof*, *The Rose Tattoo*, *The Sound of Music*, *The Goodbye Girl*, *Paper Moon*, and *The Fantasticks*. Many fans of all ages recognize Lea as the singing voice of Princess Jasmine from *Aladdin* and Fa Mulan for *Mulan* and *Mulan II*. In honor of her portrayal of the beloved princesses, the Walt Disney Company bestowed the honor of "Disney Legend" to Lea in August of 2011.

NIC CORY is an actor, writer, and professional acting coach living in New York City. A graduate of the Acting/Music Theatre program at Carnegie Mellon, he has performed Off-Broadway in *The Boys Upstairs*, *Signs of Life*, and *The Rocky Horror Show*. He is a member of the BMI Lehman Engel Workshop. He coaches aspiring artists—especially high school students applying to conservatory programs—through GET U. IN. Check him out at getuin.com.

MARA JILL HERMAN is a contributing writer for BroadwaySpace.com, HollandAmericaBlog.com, and *Edge* magazine, the official University of the Arts publication. A native New Yorker and UArts graduate with a BFA in Musical Theater, Mara has appeared in various regional productions and the North American tour of *Jesus Christ Superstar*. She is a 2011 recipient of the UArts Young Alumni Service Award and a past winner of the Musical Theatre Merit Award from YoungArts. Mara gives audition workshops for teens across the country. Mara and Ted have harmonized through the years in show choir and as Liesl and Rolf in *The Sound of Music*, but this is their first literary collaboration! www.MaraJillHerman.com.

To learn more about the author, contributors, and the book,
please visit www.soyouwannabeasuperstar.com.